Also by Bob Dowell

*Understanding the Bible: Head and Heart,
Part One—The Old Testament*

*Understanding the Bible: Head and Heart,
Part Two—Matthew through Acts*

*Understanding the Bible: Head and Heart,
Part Three—Romans through Revelation*

Papa, Tell Us about the Bible

Satan and Me and OBE: An Out of Body Experience

What Makes America Great

These books are available in paperback and e-book at amazon.com
and barnesandnoble.com.
For quick access type in author's name: Bob Dowell.

POEMS ABOUT THINGS
THAT MATTERED MOST

Poems About Things That Mattered Most:

Faith, Family, Country

by
Bob Dowell

© 2020 by Bob Dowell

All rights reserved. This book or any portion thereof may not be reproduced or used in any manner whatsoever without the express written permission of the publisher except for the use of brief quotations in a book review.

ISBN: 979-8-65539-114-7

Table of Contents

A Happy Birthday Memory · 1
Guidance and God's Will · 3
The Golden Anniversary of Nancy and Bob · · · · · · · · · · · · 5
To My Grandson Will Upon Reaching His Majority · · · · · · · · 11
Living Life Under the Aspect of Eternity · · · · · · · · · · · · · · 15
Why I Write about the Bible · 17
What Makes America Great · 19
Our Patriotic Dollar Bill · 21
Prescription for Adam's Fall · 23
The Great Fish That Swallows · 25
Christian versus Jew: Why So? · 31
A Tribute to Our Longtime Friend Dr. Dan on His Birthday
 Eighty-Second · 33
Meditation on Tithing · 35
Celebrating America's Greatness · · · · · · · · · · · · · · · · · · · 37
Cotton Mather's Passion for the Exemplary · · · · · · · · · · · · 39
A Patriot Looks at America · 41
The English Bible: Translation and Revolution · · · · · · · · · · 51
Ben Franklin's Exemplary Stand · 61
Another Look at America's Greatness · · · · · · · · · · · · · · · · 63
Jonathan Edwards, Man of Zeal · 67
Jefferson: The Declaration and the Exemplary · · · · · · · · · · 69
The Sacrament of Communion · 71
Walking with Mary: In Nazareth, in Bethlehem, in Jerusalem · · · · · 73
Gideon Then and Now · 81
My Unforgettable Bird Dogs Lou and Ike · · · · · · · · · · · · · · 87
Nanny and Papa Meet Allison · 91
Santa's Christmas Gift Story · 93
To Nancy on Christmas 2012 · 95
Meditation on Brenda's Birthday Fifty · · · · · · · · · · · · · · · · 97

To Colton James on His Eighteenth Birthday	99
To My Grandson Colton on His Nineteenth Birthday	101
Happy Mother's Day to My Wife	103
The Story of Mighty Enron	105
Bidding 2001 Adieu	107
Grandkids Can Teachers and Healers Be	111
Motherhood, a Universal Phenomenon	113
I Can't Believe Hailey Is Sixteen!	115
A Look at Islam	117
The Coronavirus Pandemic of 2020 and More	123
Things That Matter Most	125
Cale, Remembering You on Your Thirtieth Birthday	127
Remembering When…	131
Our Great-Grands Visit the Farm	133
Author Biography	135

About This Little Book

Having celebrated my eighty-seventh birthday and in a reminiscent mood, I ventured into my memento-filled attic to take a look around. Foremost among the things that caught my attention were the stacks of folders containing poems that I had written over the years addressing this occasion or that occasion, this issue or that issue, this reflection or that reflection. As I scanned poem after poem, it occurred to me that subconsciously I had attempted to preserve samples of "things that really mattered" in my life. And to do so, I had attempted through poetry to freeze in time these experiences so they would live as long as the poems lived.

As I continued reading poem after poem, thoroughly enjoying reliving a variety of experiences that had particularly mattered in the ebb and flow of my life, I began to wonder if other readers might not enjoy reading these poems. No doubt that they can identify with the subject categories—faith, family, and country—I reasoned. Then why not share them? Why not collect a few dozen in book form and publish them? So here they are in this little book!

As you will note in the table of contents, the collection is varied. It features biblical persons and events; American leaders and events; special family celebrations such as Christmas, Mother's Day, birthdays, anniversaries; and a few philosophical and theological meditations. Some of the poems are lengthy; some are short; some are in between. Some are narrative; some are lyrical; some are both narrative and lyrical. Whichever, all strive to relate to both head and heart in order to communicate a felt understanding of the subject. All strive to communicate the subject as something to experience, as something more than information. That is to say, they all strive to connect conviction of mind with consent of heart.

If a certain poem does not appeal to you, please move on to another one. Since there are many, you can be selective. So feast on the ones that fulfill. And may you feast bountifully!

—Bob Dowell

A Happy Birthday Memory

To my wife on her eighty-fourth birthday

Flashback to the beginning (1957)…

…of a relationship never ending (2019).

The year was 1957; the place, East Texas State Howdy Dance.
Coeds galore, but the one in tight-fitting green held my glance.
Luckily, my friend Joe Wayne discerned why I was so entranced
And, smiling, said, "That's the girl I told you about yesterday.
She's an Apache Bell from TJC and quite a stepper, they say,
So let's go over and say howdy before she's whisked away."
Little did I dream that coed in green would soon be my wife,
But love at first sight soon bonded us in marriage for life.
Then, seemingly in no time, the kids came and went;
Likewise our teaching careers, then retirement.
And now age on our body and brow begins to show,
But happily our memories never age; that I know.
Memories of that coed in the tight-fitting green
Enter my mind looking exactly as then seen.
No matter I am eighty-six and you today eighty-four.
We are blessed with a love that transcends, and more;
We are blessed with a love that never ever goes away.
And on that blessed note, I wish you a happy birthday.

Guidance and God's Will

A metaphor emerges.

It is well known that we need *guidance* in doing the will of God,
But that guidance need not take the form of a punishing rod.
When I look at the letters in *guidance*, the word *dance* jumps out at me,
And a metaphor comes to mind about music and steps and harmony.
In a sense, you see, dancing can be compared to doing God's will
For both involve two beings striding together as in a choreographed drill.
If both try to lead, nothing comes out right,
Be it day, or be it night.
It's only when one takes the lead with gentle cues that harmony begins.
Together in rhythm and step, each compliments the other like bookends,
And at its best, it's as if the two become one body gliding perfectly
For now they're a team, each doing what's required for compatibility.
The dance requires willing surrender and attentiveness from one;
As for the other, gentle and skillful guidance is the thing done.
Putting my dance metaphor on hold, I look at the letters in *guidance* once more.
And lo, again I see something most striking, something I did not see before:
The *g* is God, followed by *u* and *i*, thus completing my metaphor perfectly.
The *u* and *i* following God spell out the dance of life when done rightly.
Now, allow me to state explicitly what so far has only been implied:
Allowing God to lead perfects our own will without his being denied.

The Golden Anniversary of Nancy and Bob

Dr. Bob entertains family and friends by humorously recounting a bit of biographical history of the couple's fifty years of marriage.

Fifty years ago in Tyler, Texas, who would have thunk it
Of two East Texas college kids uniting in a marriage junket,
Hayseeds in their hair and probably holes in their underwear?
No one saw gold for this couple starting out that cold January night drear,
Yet the two were imbued with fortitude from a life of hardscrabble on the land.
With that and prayer and a couple of college degrees, they set out hand in hand.
First to Colorado to a little mountain town to educate its urchins despite snow and ice.
Though it was hardscrabble all over again, these hardy mountain people were very nice.
But Bob could not shake off his professorial dreams and constantly talked of higher degrees.
It sounded a bit ludicrous as he helped Nancy hang out diapers on the line to instantly freeze.

Though Stan was now potty trained, Dwight had just arrived, hardly a week ahead of Santa Claus.

School was not in session—it was Christmas vacation—but for Bob and Nancy, there was no pause.

Nancy was busy being Supermom, and Bob helped some when there were no graduate school catalogs around.

And sure enough, as the spring semester ended and the snow and ice melted, the Dowells were Denver bound.

They found a basement apartment with a backyard for the boys to play and Bob to grow veggies and things green.

Nancy taught elementary school while Bob kept the boys by day and went to school at night pursuing his dream.

Soon, with a graduate fellowship in hand, Bob was able to move the family into university housing, above ground.

The dorm for married couples at DU was quite a step up from hardscrabble on the farm or a basement apartment:

Nancy a nice job; the boys good day care; Bob time for the library. The days at DU were days of contentment.

Time went along without major incident, though Stan and Dwight once played a frightening game with the refrigerator.

Stan, being taller, could reach the door handle and could get Dwight out, but when Dwight's turn came, he could not reach the door.

So he runs to where his dad is reading, as usual, and screams, "Daddy, Daddy, Stan's in the fridge!"

Looking up, Bob spoke firmly but did not shout: "Tell Stan to get out of that fridge, and stay out!"

But the panic-stricken eyes of Dwight prevail, and the words "Stan's in the fridge" take on meaning literal.

Stan was literally in the fridge with door closed tight, and the handle too high for little Dwight.

But all in all, things went well, and Bob and Nancy and Stan and Dwight lived happily in relationship tight.

Seemingly soon, at least for Bob, the classes were finished, the dissertation completed and defended, too,

And Stan and Dwight running through the dorm, announcing, "My daddy's one too; he's a doctor daddy like you."
With the PhD in hand, the Dowells, now four instead of two, head back to Texas, to ETSU happily.
Bob has his pipe and sweater with leather elbow pads; his professorial dream had become reality.
Nancy opens her own private school—Kiddie College, it was called, filled with professors' kids ages four and five.
Stan and Dwight now had friends galore coming to Kiddie College next door, always keeping things live.
Adult social life was interesting, too, especially with Nancy active in the ladies' Newcomers Faculty Club.
Commerce, Texas, like most small college towns, was for the region the cultural beacon and social hub.
Nancy thought the Dowell family was settled in for good, Bob happily professing, and hunting too.
Besides being a professor, he had another obsession: hunting quail behind his bird dog named Lou,
Though old Lou was only one of several he had trained on the ag lands owned by East Texas State.
Training dogs and hunting quail was fun but much more fun was finding quail and shooting straight.
Walking for hours without a covey scent was discouraging for both Professor Bob and bird dog Lou,
But miles of fruitless walking gave Bob time to think the problem through, perceiving what best to do.
He knew there were quail galore in the dry land approaching the Rio Grande, and a little college too.
He also knew that colleges sorely needed PhDs after getting tons of offers when graduating in 1962.
And would it not be educational for the family to live in a multicultural region, as well as for old Lou?
Before working it all out, old Lou had passed on to happier hunting grounds, leaving young Ike in her place.

And in the fall of 1967, the Dowells and Ike made their way to McAllen soon to compete with Beulah for space.
Despite the educational experience of riding out a hurricane, Nancy began to question the move
And informed husband Bob that any more of his educational whims must first by her be approved.
But after the sun came out and the waters receded and we reclaimed our house, things turned around.
School out, Stan and Dwight entertained friends; Ike and Bob found quail prolific on all the high ground;
And Nancy thrived relating by phone and letter her narrative entitled "Riding Out the Hurricane."
But bigger than Beulah was the discovery of First United Methodist Church at Cedar and Main.
As a family we joined the congregation, and after some thirty-five years Nancy and Bob still remain.
And so does our daughter Brenda, our third child, born here in McAllen soon after our move down.
Stan moved on, finding spouse Sally in Houston town; Dwight found friend Jeanna in Dallas town.
Brenda found spouse Jimmy right here at Lake James, but little did he know what was in store,
How for his in-laws, he would be hosting birthday parties and wedding anniversaries and more.
How fortunate are Bob and Nancy to have Brenda and Jimmy, Dwight and Jeanna, Sally and Stan.
Needless to say, this couple of fifty years consider themselves a most fortunate woman and man.
With loving children and their spouses and so many friends gathered here to celebrate their anniversary gold,
And let us not forget our grandchildren: Will and Cale, Colton and Macy, and Hailey and Lori, grandchildren all told.
What could be more golden for a couple of fifty years than to be surrounded by loving children, in-laws, and friends?

Bob and Nancy want to say, "Thank you all for honoring us, and thank you Lord above for making life so good. Amen."

To My Grandson Will Upon Reaching His Majority

Viewing my first grandson elicited a feeling between awe and thrill;
I gazed at a little seven-pound guy all diapered and dressed called Will.
I thought of holding you before glancing toward your most protective Mom
And sensed a mother daring anyone to violate the space of her infant son.
So I took off the germ protective viewing mask and began my patient wait
Thinking that when Mom grew weary, around her I would stealthily navigate.
You must have been nearing two when I finally got to hold you:
Baby Cale was crying, the phone was ringing, and the doorbell too.
But one could do worse than inherit protective parents always hovering near
And at a distance is, no doubt, the appropriate place for grandparents to steer
Though Papa and Nanny* did steal you away a time or two and take you to the farm
Where you helped your great-grandfather feed cows, fix fences and stock the barn.
*[grandfather and grandmother were known as Papa and Nanny]
And you did quite well: a little urbanite who adapted to agrarian life readily
Just like later at Kanakuk's summer camp, you adapted to primitive living easily.
Before I realized I was a grandfather you were graduating from Second Baptist High:

Time's winged chariot had sped on; you now eighteen and no longer the little guy.
You put on burnt orange and headed for awesome UT intent on earning a degree.
Time's winged chariot had hurried on, pushing you into majority and me to seventy.
Oh, to be twenty-one again and aware of Time's winged chariot always hurrying near!
Of course, that cannot be except through fantasy: so grandson Will, lend me your ear.
When I was twenty-one my grandfather said to me, "Ever notice the sun at its zenith?"
"Oh sure, when I look up at noon," I replied wondering where all this might leadeth.
"Now, think of one day's course of the sun as one life time," said grandfather to grandson.
"Then think of sunrise as birth, midday as midlife, and sunset as life done," he continued on.
"You, grandson, are about half way between sunrise and midday; when you look at the sun
You see the sun only at its zenith and so seeing see only one side of life's arc, the upside one.
What I'm saying grandson is that the course of the sun is an arc like the course of life is an arc.
Note, I'm speaking metaphorically, for indirect communication is more likely to leave its mark.
You are now one and twenty and well on your way to midday where you will see life's bent,
For standing on the zenith you also see the downside of the arc, the sunset side of the event."
"Glimpsing the downside of the arc ushers wisdom in, for time becomes precious then.
The sunset side instantly illuminates a new perspective; it gives new meaning to 'when.'

As finiteness sinks in, prioritizing begins; it is the only defense against the fast moving sun.
Either we devour time or time devours us; so let us set our priorities, each and every one.
We cannot stop the sun; we can only prioritize our lives, and in doing so *we* make *him* run."
So grandson Will, please ponder this philosophical metaphor now that you are twenty-one.

Living Life Under the Aspect of Eternity

Perspective determines our state of mind
Thinking eternal adds perspective divine
Death becomes a beginning, not an end
God becomes more important than man.
Heaven and Hell become a reality
It's one or the other ultimately.
The choice is ours to make
We decide which route to take
The road to Heaven or the road to Hell
Belief leads to Heaven, unbelief to Hell.
So says the Bible, and says it oh so well.
Now, I ask you to answer this question honestly:
Are, you, living life under the aspect of eternity?
If your answer is yes, I say a hearty amen!
If your answer is no, I say consider again!

Why I Write about the Bible

Besides teaching and quail hunting, Dr. Bob has a third obsession: writing. Except for a few articles, he put his writing on hold until retirement from university teaching. Since his retirement at the beginning of the year 2000, he has been writing books about the Bible.

Author Bob Dowell, PhD

Why do you write about the Bible, I'm sometimes quizzed?
My answer: because it's the most important book there is!
It answers the basic questions that everyone should ask:
What is the purpose of life? Why am I here? What is my task?
The answer to those basic questions comes from God above,
Who "breathed' words in Bible form and delivered with love.
Genesis to Revelation addresses life's purpose again and again,
Revealing how the world began and how the world will end,
Defining right and wrong and the terrible consequences of sin
Lest by grace through faith it is overcome: our salvation, amen!
One thing more! You're invited to meet my book family on Amazon.
They welcome the opportunity to share the Bible with all who come.

What Makes America Great

Let's speculate on what makes America great:
Reverence for the Bible carries the most weight;
In God We Trust is on our currency stamped strong
To let the world know we seek right over wrong.
All persons are created equal in pursuit of happiness;
This self-evident truth our Declaration gives witness.
US history reveals that when equality goes amiss,
A great leader steps forward to lead the redress.
Stanton issues the Declaration of Sentiments,
Declaring equality for women a priority event.
Lincoln guides us through the Civil War, slavery to end,
Emancipation Proclamation, Gettysburg Address, amen.
Then M. L. King Jr. with "I Have a Dream" the nation assails,
And through mighty rhetoric, civil rights reform propels.
So it has been and may it continue to be
In God We Trust that guides our country.

Our Patriotic Dollar Bill

Suggestion to the reader: place a dollar bill in front of you to reference as you read this poem.

In God We Trust is engraved on all our currency explicitly,
And the ubiquitous dollar bill expresses our faith implicitly.
There revealed is our founders' providential view
That America was predestined as the chosen new
To embody the noble ideal of Western civilization:
A biblically oriented people, a God-fearing nation.
On its front and back, images inscribed collectively
All scripted succinctly and encrypted figuratively
America predestined to be great, to be exemplary.
On the back the Great Seal, its obverse and reverse
Above the unfinished pyramid, the Eye of Providence, emphatic
Eye and unfinished pyramid capped by a Latin phrase prophetic:
annuit coeptis, meaning "God approves our undertaking."
The thirteen layers of unfinished pyramid—there is no mistaking
Thirteen layers, thirteen colonies that became the thirteen states,
Thirteen colonies, then thirteen states that became the United States,
Represented by the ancient symbol of strength and permanence,
The pyramid, and guided and approved by the Eye of Providence.
On the bottom layer of the pyramid is the founding date,
There inscribed in Roman numerals—1776, they translate.
The Latin phrase placed beneath the pyramid by our sages,
Novus ordo seclorum, translates "the new order of the ages,"
Meaning the exemplary USA being the new order designate
Stated in Latin, then the universal language of church and state.
The obverse of the Great Seal images the bald eagle and his shield USA

Lined with thirteen red and white stripes, the thirteen colonies of the day
Later becoming the thirteen states, foundation of the exemplary USA.
To confirm, the eagle holds a banner in its beak with Latin phrase thereon:
E pluribus unum, reads the banner inscription, meaning "out of many one."
The olive branch in the eagle's right talon suggests peace requested,
But the bundle of arrows in the left talon suggests strength if tested.
Above the head of the eagle a constellation of thirteen stars swirl,
Indicating a new nation taking its place among nations of the world.
So there on the dollar bill, you view the highly symbolic Great Seal,
The reverse and obverse, the pyramid and eye, the eagle and shield,
Latin phrases, the number thirteen, and symbols unending,
All selected to glorify our nation and its blessed beginning.
So now that we know the message encrypted implicitly on the patriotic dollar bill,
Let it be our cue: *annuit coeptis*, "God approves our undertaking," our prayer still.

Prescription for Adam's Fall

In Adam's fall we sinned all: our heritage sad.
God's paradisiacal plan suddenly went bad
When rebel Satan entered Eden, revenge in mind,
Determined to destroy newly created mankind,
Angel turned rogue and from Heaven banned,
Now living only to harass both God and man.
Do not be deceived about the forbidden fruit, he tells Eve.
The truth is you will become godlike: deceived, she believes.
The fruit so good to her taste, she convinces Adam to participate;
Thus done, paradise fades away, leaving humanity in a fallen state.
Satan struck a mighty blow against God and humanity for sure,
But God was not to be outdone by the evil one; he had a cure.
It's called redemption, and the prescription is available to everyone.
Stated simply and clear: by grace through faith, salvation will come.
Though Eden faded, Satan stayed on, stalking the earth to and fro,
Ever the sly serpent deceiving descendants of Adam and Eve: lo!
Happily, however, fear not if the Bible you truly believe:
"Submit yourself to God, resist old Satan and he will flee!" (James 4:7).

The Great Fish That Swallows

This poem comprises a portion of the Jonah commentary in my book "Understanding the Bible: Head and Heart—Part One, The Old Testament."

What is the great fish that swallows the prophet Jonah of Israel?
Figuratively, it operates outside the sea; thus, it cannot be a whale.
Figuratively, it is the consuming bias of exclusiveness,
Accepting only Abraham's descendants for inclusiveness.
Jonah abhors God's call to prophesy to Nineveh, the Gentile city;
For those unholy foreigners he could not conjure up an ounce of pity.
He could not forget those arrogant Assyrians of old
Who came down like a wolf on the fold,
Savagely attacking Jerusalem the sacred city of Israel.
How could God now call an Israelite to save them from hell?
Jonah had rather die than see wicked Nineveh repent;
The thought of preaching to Assyrians put him in a snit.
Thus, he jogs down to Joppa and boards a ship to Tarshish,
The opposite direction from Nineveh on the Tigris.
Prophet or no, Jonah flees like a repulsed lover;
Descending deep inside the ship, he takes cover.
But God will have none of that;
He calls up a storm to frighten the little rat.
The mariners do all they can to stay the storm;
They pray to their gods and sound the alarm
While Jonah dozes deep in the hold of the ship.
He was in a suicide mode; he didn't give a flip.
Awakened, he confesses he is the cause,
But his refusal to pray gives the mariners pause.
Very reluctantly, they toss Jonah into the sea
After he confesses, "The tempest is because of me."

Then, seeing the sea becoming calm and nice,
The mariners, in awe, offer vows and sacrifice
While suicidal Jonah experiences further woe.
God is not about to let the rascal go.
He prepares a great fish to swallow Jonah whole;
He would teach this rebel prophet to be so bold.
But just how much Jonah relents is subject to debate.
True, a sanctimonious prayer he does relate,
Yet within the dark and spongy belly of the fish,
He seems to secretly harbor his original hateful wish.
No doubt the fish is sickened by this hateful little man
For after three days, he vomits him up onto dry land.
But Jonah did learn one thing about obedience to God:
You do what he says, or he wields his rod.
So Jonah obeys when God a second time gives his nod.
Though somewhat morose, toward Nineveh he does trod.
But before we trod further with this despicable little dude,
Let us step back and look for influences that may feed his hateful attitude.
This prophet, hateful or not, can hardly be unfamiliar with his cultural state
And thus could have gleaned certain criteria to feed his prejudice-filled pate.
Perhaps he remembers instructions for conquering the evil Canaanites:
Destroy both cities and inhabitants so as not to be seduced by their ungodly rites.
Perhaps he remembers the cruel Gentile empires that toyed with his tiny state.
Recalling the abuse by Egypt and Assyria would certainly be enough to irritate.
Perhaps he is too puffed with his chosen people status as Abraham's descendant
To ever fully realize that he is chosen not to be exalted but to ever be the servant.

Jonah is no Isaiah, nor was meant to be; he wore blinders and could not fully see.
Jonah is provincial; unlike the visionary Isaiah, he refuses to see universally.
He shares not Isaiah's insight that God chose Israel as a light to the Gentile world.
No, he conveniently writes off the foreigner as an unrighteous, unworthy churl.
He conveniently ignores the covenant and Abraham's example as guides.
He conveniently chooses to be provincial and flow with the local tides.
He conveniently choses to exclude rather than include.
In short, he conveniently chooses to be a hateful little dude.
But let us not in condemning old Jonah fall into a self-righteous pit.
He may be provincial, but his problem is universal writ.
The Jonah lesson is a biblical lesson that has to be taught again and again,
Perhaps most effectively in the parable of the Good Samaritan,
A parable that dramatically teaches compassion and inclusion,
That oh so soundly condemns hate and exclusion.
Is this message not also that of the book of Jonah, one the prophet chose to ignore,
Despite God's exertions to bring his prophet's unexercised compassion to the fore?
But this discrepancy is all well and good, for it's an effective literary device;
It's called dramatic irony, and it underscores the theme of the story twice.
Let me illustrate from the story so that you can really see
And, of course, in the future a more perceptive reader be.
Not daring to overtly disobey God a second time, Jonah trod toward the great city.
Even though his agenda was not God's agenda, he remained a prophet without pity.
There is no "if" in his message: "Forty days and Nineveh shall be destroyed."

Should Nineveh opt to repent, this prophet would obviously be most annoyed.
Ironically, the king exhorts his people to put on sackcloth and cry mightily to God,
Triggering Jonah's worst fear: that merciful Yahweh will hear and spare the rod.
Angrily, Jonah cries to God: "Did I not tell you so when in my own country?"
I know your loving kindness, your slowness to anger, and how merciful you can be.
Must I witness for forty days while a horde of hated Gentiles find favor in your sight?
Lord, to this prophet that would be a hateful, heinous sight; it is unjust; it is not right!"
I ask you, reader, is there a discrepancy here between what is and what should be?
There most certainly is, and the literary device employed is called dramatic irony.
It is the device that enhances understanding through the use of subtle psychology.
It provides the reader perspective to see what the character should but does not see,
Thus boldly underscoring the thematic concern of the piece of work.
Here, it underscores the fact that Jonah the prophet is, without doubt, a jerk.
To a foreign neighbor, he can show neither love nor mercy of any fashion,
Yet God keeps patience with this petulant prophet, hoping for a hint of compassion.
As one last strategy, God employs analogy on the stubborn son of a gun
For purposes of cooling his anger and shading him from the burning sun.
The Lord causes a plant to grow up overnight to protect the little bum.
But he also prepares a worm to destroy the plant overnight.

Grateful for the plant but outraged when the worm comes into sight,
Jonah again wishes to die; he says the preparing of the worm was not right!
Through analogy, God tries to tap the sympathy of his hateful little foe:
He reminds Jonah of his own pity for the plant he cherishes so.
"Why should I," says God, "not likewise have pity on Nineveh, this great city
Filled with thousands of children innocent as a kitty?"
Is God's analogy on this stiff-necked, stubborn prophet lost?
Probably so: ironically, Jonah seems determined to hate Nineveh at any cost.
But is the story's irony lost on the reader, you and me?
Not so; we know how its irony communicates just what the author wants us to see;
We also know its irony communicates its theme the most effective way: implicitly.
But to review, let us state it explicitly: *'tis folly to allow consuming bias to swallow us.*
Now, have we not learned to read the book of Jonah, understanding all its fuss?
Have we not learned that focusing on the story's irony is an absolute must?
Have we not learned to perceive the irony of all the story's carefully designed parts?
And could it be that we, ironically, have discovered Jonah living in our own hearts?

CHRISTIAN VERSUS JEW: WHY SO?

Being Christian, must you hate the Jew?
For centuries that seemed the thing to do.
Christ killers, Jews were called, guilty all,
Thereby subject to atrocities that appall
Until common sense responds with question,
Asking, did Judaism not Christianity spawn?
Christians, do you not know Jesus was a Jew?
So were the first Christians, Peter and Paul, too.
God chose faithful Abraham and covenant made,
But his Israelite descendants their God dismayed.
Except for a few prophets, and maybe King David,
The Israelites more often than not made God livid.
The testament old tells you how the story goes,
Relating a few episodes of joy but more of woe.
After Adam's fall and Noah's flop, Abraham was called,
He and his Israelite descendants to model God's will for all.
Despite models like Moses and Joshua, plus the Decalogue,
The stiff-necked Israelites mostly stumbled as if inside a fog.
Obey law and the covenant seemingly they could not do,
So, as Jeremiah prophesied, God devised a covenant new.[1]
Then sent his Son in human form, it perfectly to unfold,
A new covenant to fulfill the law and to complete the old.
Jesus in Matthew[2] says so, and the gospel genealogies reveal:
Perfect life, cross and resurrection, law and covenant to fulfill.
Reasonably, Christians could want Jews Christians to become
But to hate and want to persecute the Jews: unjust and dumb.

1　See Jeremiah 31:31–34.

2　See Matthew 5:17.

There would be no Christians had the Jews not paved the way,
And who can say Jews will not be embraced on Judgment Day?
After conversion, it was a gnawing concern of the apostle Paul,
A Jew, but the resurrected Jesus to convert the Gentiles called.[3]
In a graft metaphor, Paul warns Gentiles the Jews not condemn:
They were the tree's natural branches; you only the grafted limb.[4]
Keep in mind that you do not support the root, but the root you
And the Creator could in the future graft the natural branch anew.
So, Christian, since the Creator is the potter and you are the clay,
Would it not be wiser, rather than hate the Jews, for them pray?

---

3 See Acts 9:15.
4 See Romans 9:17–21.

A Tribute to Our Longtime Friend Dr. Dan on His Birthday Eighty-Second

In 1967 the Dowell family moved to McAllen, there a long time to be
Bob, a professor at PAC, and Nancy, a preschool director at McAllen ISD.
Settled in at 1208 La Vista, we began our search of a new church home.
Being from different denominations, we thought best a neutral tone.
After visitation and family deliberation, it was FUMC[5] that we settled on.
The children said, "The FUMC youth program is great fun!"
Bob and Nancy said, "The FUMC Friendship class is number one!"
For the class was led by none other than the charismatic Dr. Dan,
Who applied biblical directive to social issues affecting his fellow man.
Inside the church and outside the church, duly dedicated Dr. Dan led with zeal,
Prime directives, love the Lord and love your neighbor, he demonstrated for real.
When there was need in the church or in the community,
Dr. Dan always saw the occasion a Christian opportunity.
Occasion after occasion, he stepped forward, stepped forward and led.
Like the biblical James, he believed faith without works to be dead.
And he not only led; he demonstrated creative flair while he led:
As stewardship chair, he posed a rhetorical question that to this day remains alive.
The living question: "Did you ever hear of a person going broke because he tithed?"

---

5 First United Methodist Church.

I could go on and on, but I know that brevity is usually best,
So, for the time being, I shall give my praise prone pen a rest—
But not before I relate one short anecdote to praise my longtime friend:
On our first FUMC visit, near the annex stood an imposing elderly man, Mr. Lennard
(A name we learned that children sometimes misconstrued, calling him "the Lord").
Smiling, he reached out to Nancy and me, and to the friendship class we were taken;
But unlike the speaker in Frost's poem, who in later life pined about the road not taken,
I thank "the Lord" for showing us the road that led to years of friendship with Dr. Dan,
Not only a friend but a mentor, too, in his exemplary service to God and fellow man.

Meditation on Tithing

Is it possible that I a robber could be?
What I read in Malachi disturbs me.[6]
He tells the Israelites they are robbing God.
They give the prophet a vigorous no-no nod.
"Oh yes," says he, "my accusation is true;
In holding back tithes and offerings, you do!"
Oh my, think I, is not this something I do too?
It is a thought that chills me through and through.
So I read more, hoping to find a solution to my crime,
And there it is in black and white, and just in time!
The Israelites are told: "Bringing the whole tithe in
For filling the Lord's storehouse is his command."
The prophet then challenges the people to put God to the test.
"First, fill his storehouse, and you will be the one blessed!"[7]
Thanks to Malachi, I know now what I must do:
I must think of tithing as essential worship too.

---

6 See Malachi 3:8–9.
7 See Malachi 3:10.

Celebrating America's Greatness

What Makes America Great book signing at Barnes & Noble

Is it not time to celebrate what makes America great?
To stay the negative and on the positive concentrate?
Come with me on a brief tour of literature and history
To review why America is great as it was meant to be
If we hold to the principles our founders held adamantly:
That for a commonweal to endure it must God directed be.
That does not mean a theocracy, church and state combined,
But a Bible-oriented populace who believe in a higher mind,
A Creator divine who created design and governs by design.
Obedience to the Creator's design releases blessing divine.
Thus, America as the "city upon a hill" emits exemplary shine,
Thereby reaping rich blessings despite slips from time to time.
Now, come with me and meet a few of America's most exemplary
Founding fathers and exhorters whose actions shaped our history.
Dear reader, a little information to entice you to come along:
This is not a big thick book filled with tedious detail prolong.

What Makes America Great can be read in just one sitting or two;
It's succinctly narrated to inform and entertain without tiring you.

"*What Makes America Great*" *is available online at Amazon and Barnes & Noble.*

COTTON MATHER'S PASSION FOR THE EXEMPLARY

Cotton Mather (1663–1728): New England Puritan clergyman; also scientist as well as a prolific and influential author

Cotton Mather, prodigy from heaven,
Entered Harvard[8] at the age of eleven.
Passionately served his community,
Always focused on the exemplary.
And though he lived in an earlier century,
His concerns might well apply to you and me.
Lamenting the loss of godly zeal in the old Bay Colony,
He put his defensive pen to paper incessantly,
Preparing four-hundred-plus instructive works for delivery.
He declared that New England must live, at least, in our history.
Calling on his heavenly muse, he penned a prose epic grand,
Telling how his Puritan ancestors, newly chosen ones, came to this land,
How Providence showered their act with holy blessedness,
And how divine power and wisdom radiated a wilderness.
The epic records the exemplary lives of Puritan leaders in the main;
Magnalia Christi Americana is its Latin name.
Viewing the New England of Winthrop and Bradford,
Mather readily found many godly, exemplary lives to record.
But turning to his contemporaries for a like sample,
Degeneration was more likely to be the example.
"Surely something can be done to stay this unraveling of the good,"
Thinks Mather, adamantly determined to do whatever he could.
First, he set about being good and exhorted others to do the same,

---

8 Harvard was founded by the Massachusetts Bay Colony Puritans in 1636.

Instructing all the while that being good meant self-denial.
And for the record, he revealed an instance of himself on trial.
He confessed his desire for "a young gentlewoman of incomparable carriage,"
A spirited celebrity who aggressively offered herself to minister Mather in marriage.
Yet since her reputation lay under a certain disadvantage, or so the claim,
Family and congregation informed minister Mather such a marriage was insane.
Knowing that Satan was working to destroy the Mather pastorship,
He prays fervently that his God not let him slip.
He fasted and prayed and threw himself prostrate on his study floor,
Imploring God to help him find a way, on the devil's temptation, to close the door.
The miracle came in the form of a neighbor, a widow of peerless reputation,
Welcomed by Mather and approved by God, family, and congregation.
But Mather always knew that being good was only half the equation;
Serving God meant serving others; there was simply no evasion.
And this cardinal principle Mather worked desperately to communicate,
Hoping to advance the good but the negative to abate.
Again, this godly Harvard graduate takes his prolific pen in hand
And through the "do good" essays appeals to the exemplary in man,
No matter what his adversarial critics say;
Mather with his pen helped save the day
By recording the early New England way
Permanently in our country's history.

A Patriot Looks at America

I found the 9/11 terrorist attacks a 911 call for all Americans to examine their heritage for solace and direction. The following verses are the result of my own examination and are dedicated to my fellow patriots.

Viewing contemporary America and its history,
I find few things shrouded in cloudy mystery.
Its good deeds and its bad deeds are exposed for all to see,
And that characteristic is one of the many things that impresses me.
Comparatively, I believe my country has earned a very special place
In the storied chapters, ancient or modern, of the human race.
I realize the America that I love is far from being a perfect country,
Yet I appreciate the early Puritan view that it was meant to be.
And being of nostalgic sway, I'm inclined to agree.
I certainly do believe that it was more than economic greed
That motivated the Bay Colony and the Plymouth Plantation breed.
Their literature and history, filled with religious zeal, is there for all to read.
Europe had teemed with religious zeal for a century or more,
The result of the Reformation's volcanic spiritual fervor.
Translators, theologians, and sects sprang up by the scores,
Spreading their new beliefs beyond the continent's shores.
Bibles, now translated into their own vernacular and clutched in hand,
Many saints[9] sailed west determined to root their perceptions in a new land.
It has been said that America's roots are planted in the Bible.
I, for one, believe that statement to be, in the main, reliable.

---

9 The Puritans used the word *saints* to refer to believers in Jesus Christ, as sometimes used in the New Testament. See Romans 1:7.

When I think of our country's beginning, I think of the *Mayflower* arriving,
Bringing weary Pilgrims to continue their courageous striving,
Who, so determined to pursue their religious inclination,
Separated themselves from their former church and nation.
I also think of Winthrop and his Puritan cohorts bold
Aboard the *Arbella*, awaiting to land and play their role.
As their governor to be, he outlines the script in a sermon sublime,
Reminding his group that they are players in a drama divine:
They are the New Israelites in a covenant relationship with God,
Obligating them to follow the Lord's will or to rue his rod.
They are reminded as chosen ones they have responsibilities awesome:
In the New World wilderness, they must build the New Jerusalem.
Desiring confirmation of their efforts to achieve such a grand design,
They examined every phenomenon, carefully looking for a sign divine.
Each event, large or small, that occurred anywhere under the sky
Was viewed as a possible providential message to sanction and ratify.
Whether Bradford, in his Plymouth history, recording a special work of Providence,
Or Johnson, in his prose epic, catapulting the Bay Colony into cosmic imminence,
Or Winthrop, in his journal, recounting bits of phenomena evidencing divine sanction,
These believers in the Calvinist concept of the elect found confirmation for their action.
They believed themselves New Israelites charged with an awesome commission:
Establishing a model community in the American wilderness, their divine mission.
As Winthrop so aptly stated, it was to be a city upon a hill for the world to see;
It was to be in the New World, and it was to be the example for the world to be.
Worship was to be like that prescribed in the New Testament epistles;

Law was to be modeled mainly on Old Testament sanctions, despite their bristles.
It was the Puritans' duty, they believed, to correct the church's errors of the past;
It was their covenant duty as newly chosen ones, to purify ecclesia at last.
Perhaps I have covered ground a bit too fast and depended too heavily on allusion,
So allow me to slow the pace by practicing less compression and more infusion.
Why have I focused on the Bay Colony and Plymouth Plantation?
Because there we surely find the deepest pilings of our nation.
It seems that in these two plantations our deepest roots are found,
Rather than the earlier settled Virginia colony at Jamestown.
The Jamestown arrivals were really not so filled with religious zeal,
Though they arrived first and came from the same commonweal.
Yet these adventurers came hoping to find riches galore,
For their bent of mind was more that of the conquistador.
To be sure, they quoted scripture from the current popular Geneva translation,
Respected church and clergy, but themselves felt little sense of covenant obligation.
They came not to the New World with intent to establish a city upon a hill.
They were more cavalier: adventure, riches, and status was their appeal.
It was later that Virginia plays a major role in carrying out the great enterprise,
When future leaders like Patrick Henry, Jefferson, and Washington began to rise.
Meanwhile, Bradford governed his Plymouth Pilgrims for almost two score years,
Shepherding them by the lights of the Bible and sharing in their joys and tears.
He felt sure that he and his Pilgrims were engaged in a grand design,

And a record of the divine plantings of his early plantation he left behind.
In plain style, his history reveals heroic deeds of a people engaged in battle royal
Against wilderness wilds, Satan's wiles, human depravity, and stubborn soil.
Charitable, wise, and kind, Bradford always led his Pilgrims by example
And left for posterity an exemplary guide: the first Thanksgiving a sample.
Following Bradford's Pilgrims, a decade later came John Winthrop, leading by hand
His fellow Puritans while reminding them of their obligation to the divine plan.
He might have been Moses instructing the Israelites, posed before the promised land,
Warning them all that disobedience triggers God's condemning curses on man
But that obedience frees, for everyone, showers of his bountiful blessings grand.
Consequently, the colony must the latter action embrace to fulfill the covenant plan.
In his "Model of Christian Charity" sermon, Winthrop unfolds the divine blueprint
And instructs his Puritan followers in a caring but firm tone, of the Lord's intent,
A plan involving committed persons bonded by love and bound by covenant
Who will abide by each article contained therein and walk in a straight path;
Otherwise, they would perjure themselves and cause God to break out in wrath,
For a perjured people God cannot stand: woman, child, or man.
To turn God's wrath into blessings, his people must be of one accord

And heed Micah's counsel: to do justly, love mercy, and walk humbly with the Lord,
Who shall then delight in walking with his people and in helping them to build
For all the world to see Winthrop's prophecy constructed, that "city upon a hill,"
And despite all the storms that may assault it down the years,
Allow its beacon to light our paths and to beam away our fears.
It may be said that Plymouth Plantation and Bay Colony laid the cornerstone,
Furnishing direction and foundation for succeeding generations to build upon.
Besides its native born, America has always provided countless immigrants a home,
Not always the perfect host but, even acknowledging its worst, better than most.
The exemplary motif permeates the literature and history of this great nation,
Beginning with Winthrop's model city and continuing with Jefferson's Declaration.
Of course, history reveals discrepancy between the prescribed ideal and the real,
But when evaluating, let us not forget to factor in our progress to insure a fair deal.
Martin Luther King Jr. is right when he declares "created equal" America's creed,
For history reveals that our greatest struggles, civil war and civil rights, did succeed
In activating our bedrock beliefs and in validating the morality there under seal
And in greatly narrowing the gap between the prescribed ideal and the real.
Surely America has been from its beginnings a great experiment,
Whether testing theocracy, royal colony, or democratic government.

An ocean away from Old World control, Americans felt somewhat bold;
Freed of rigid traditions, they immediately began reshaping the mold.
Reading the agenda well, our early leaders had little doubt
That they knew what the New World America was about.
Many writers have busied themselves describing the American phenomenon,
Jean de Crevecoeur, a journalist-farmer, being an early and interesting one.
In the new America, he sees industry magnificently displayed on every hand,
Reflecting the embryos of the arts, sciences, and ingenuity of many a land.
America, he observes, is truly a miraculous place, an unbelievable spot,
And rightly predicts great world changes evolving from this melting pot.
On the economic level, he praises the industry shown by the individual,
Which he gleefully explains as motivated by the principle of residual.
The individual keeps the fruits of his labor for his very own hoard
Without claim "either by a despotic prince, a rich abbot, or a mighty lord."
Religion also fares well in this new land, where various sects are settled thinly
And where frontier necessity often mixes them and renders them more friendly.
Crevecoeur made his observations when America was still colonies thirteen
But not before ominous clouds of change were appearing on the scene.
For some time, Puritan orthodoxy had been losing its sway;
Other forces were making inroads into the New England way.
Whether it would survive as a postcolonial force was a mystery,
Yet as its learned defender Mather said, "Whether or no, it must live in our history."
And Crevecoeur, rejecting fashion, maintained his own perception,
Examined the New England way, and found little that deserved rejection.

He noted their wisdom, their industry, and their love of knowledge,
Excitedly noting they established in this hemisphere the very first college.
Both their leaders and their defenders looked for the exemplary
And strived to exalt it high for all the world to see.
Though New England's preoccupation with the metaphysical did not die in the main,
It waned somewhat as secular concerns such as commerce and politics made gain.
Sam Adams of the old Bay Colony railed against taxation without representation
And led his Bostonians in staging a mammoth tea party as way of protestation.
Virginia cohort Patrick Henry chided those crying reconciliation with every breath:
No more petitions, and never chains, he cries, "Give me liberty or give me death."
Events move fast, and Paul Revere makes his famous ride a message to unfurl
For those New England farmers who fire the shot heard around the world.
Redcoats marching through the countryside to Concord and Lexington
Soon realize that the New England spirit is decidedly stubborn.
Colonial representatives from all the colonies meet in Philadelphia
To debate the disturbing question: whether to be or not to be.
The decision and the consequence did indeed try the soul;
By declaring independence, Americans were again reshaping the mold;
This time it was recorded not in sermon but in a political document;
Nevertheless, it was another city-upon-a-hill event.
It was another exemplary experiment;
It was another providential event.
To exhibit exemplary government, God chooses the American strand,
And like Winthrop, Jefferson interprets the providential plan:
People are entitled, under the laws of nature and the God of nature,

To certain inalienable rights and to protect them by legislature.
Implementing the plan is the story of America thereafter,
A story filled with much grief and struggle, and limited laughter.
We've been two centuries working out "the self-evident,"
For many chose not to face the full intent
Of that crucial line "All men are created equal."
And it's taken war, debate, and fermentation to formulate its sequel:
All people are created equal, without regard to race or gender.
Legislating thus, we now curb the would-be offender.
The women's midnineteenth century Declaration of Sentiments advised
That the equality statement of Jefferson's Declaration be strategically revised
By adding "and women" to the crucial line of this foundational document,
Dispelling any doubt of God's intent that all people share in its promised equality.
And two decades later, following a civil war, constitutional amendments evolve—
Amendments Thirteen, Fourteen, and Fifteen, the principle of equality to resolve.
Lincoln helped clarify our great exemplary experiment in his Gettysburg Address,
Which alludes to the conception of our founding fathers, to equality and its test.
Could this nation or any nation dedicated to the proposition of full equality
Long endure? It was the crucial question for our crucible condition of 1863.
It is the crucial and enduring question that echoes down the years to you and me;
It is the crucial and enduring question that continues to shape our country's history.
And so we see that America is the land of exemplary experiment,
Whether the focus be on the model community or civil government,

Whether it be the Puritans testing their faith under harsh realities,
Or whether it be the patriots testing theories of civil liberties,
Surely America is a city upon a hill established by providential decree,
Created by God, but entrusted, fellow patriot, to you and me.

The English Bible: Translation and Revolution

The following verses were composed after having read Benson Bobrick's "Wide as the Waters: The Story of the English Bible and the Revolution It Caused."

The Western world touts its greatest book, the Bible;
For all its books, the Bible has been the most reliable.
It has been the West's spiritual guide in almost every nation,
Despite extended controversy over canon and translation.
But let us not begin with a debate and end up in a stew;
Rather, let us first look at some basics as way of review.
How do we know what we know about God's word?
We often simply depend upon what we've heard,
From mother or father or Sunday school teacher,
And, of course, straight from our pulpit preacher.
But where did the clergy learn all about creation?
No doubt read it in their favorite Bible translation.
Yes, translation is a major consideration
For every person in every nation.
God's word was recorded originally in Hebrew and Greek,
Which, of course, left many tongues without God speak.
Recording is one thing, translating another;
Yet each may be thought of as the other's brother.
Recording began when old Moses started thinking things through,
His God-related experiences some scribe translated into Hebrew.
Other divinely inspired persons had their experiences recorded too;
For more than a millennium, these Hebrew testaments of old grew.
But how could descendants know who lived outside the Hebrew nation?
They could not read the inspired word without translation.
The poor wandering Jews a translation began to seek

When Alexander turned most of the known world into Greek.
Upon request, the Jerusalem high priest to Alexandria sent
Seventy-two savvy scholars to translate the Old Testament.
The result became known as the Septuagint creation,
Giving both Gentile and wandering Jew a Greek translation.
Fortunately, God's son came to a Greek-speaking world anon,
And what he said was recorded in koine, the language common.
The Gospels, Epistles, Acts, and Revelation were recorded the same
So that in a universal language, all could praise God's name—
Until the Romans changed the world with such sensation
That it became imperative to turn out a new translation.
The official language of the Roman world was, of course, Latin,
And the clergy had to use official language even for a hymn at matins.
The Septuagint version would no longer suffice;
There must be a Latin translation in every benefice.
And so it was, but poor it was, all stilted and lacking inspiration;
It was so bad that the pope finally ordered a new translation.
He called on Eusebius Hieronymus, better known as St. Jerome.
Such a linguist and biblical scholar seldom has the world known.
For two score years and more, St. Jerome labored in prayerful state
To ultimately produce, in 405 AD, the inspired Latin Vulgate.
This authorized version pleased the Church exceeding well.
It served the world until the translation of Miles Coverdale.
Since I stretched the truth to attain the previous rhyme,
I must take us back in time.
Before Coverdale, there was Tyndale challenging the norm;
And before both, there was Wycliffe pushing reform.
All three reformers were remarkable sensations,
With their unauthorized and authorized translations.
We must now slow the pace and focus on clarification:
Wycliffe, Tyndale, and Coverdale belong to the English nation.
Wycliffe is pre-Reformation, but he is definitely proreform;
His sermons seriously deviate from the Church-prescribed norm.
The Scripture he quotes creates an international sensation

For it is not the official Vulgate but his own English translation.
After almost a thousand years of the Latin Vulgate and no vernacular,
John Wycliffe's unauthorized translations were no less than spectacular.
With the help of protégé Hereford, the first Wycliffe Bible appeared in 1382;
By 1395 protégé Purvey had reworked the Vulgate to supply edition two.
Things now seemed to be in place to ensure Wycliffe's most enduring hope:
To free Christians from the "corrupt tyranny" of the pope.
Wycliffe declared that if man was to obey God's word,
He could not afford to depend only on what he heard.
Wycliffe and the church over tradition were split asunder;
Tradition must be grounded in Scripture, he would thunder.
Every man must have access to the Bible at the very least.
Later, Luther simply said, "Every man a priest."
Wycliffe's followers spread his message far and wide;
Little did they care that their name came from a snide aside:
From the word *lollen*, meaning "mumble," Lollards they were named.
No matter the derogatory tag, they spread Wycliffe's message unashamed.
For more than a century, the Lollards zealously trod the reform road,
But with limited success until the printing press caused things to explode.
On the horizon loomed the Reformation and the Renaissance,
Fomenting further revolutionary ideas to launch;
While Gutenberg technology added wings in the form of the printed word
That sped scholars' opinions around the continent to be instantly heard.
In 1452, a complete Bible rolled off the Gutenberg printer;
Soon it would be possible to supply a Bible to every saint and sinner.
The Renaissance brought the revival of classical learning and wisdom;
It spawned an intellectual movement called humanism,
Which in turn stressed the dignity of every individual

And viewed much of religious tradition as useless residual.
The Renaissance provided works not available since the fall of Rome,
Which soundly supported what the reformer Wycliffe had known:
Works like Plato's dialogues and Paul's epistles in original Greek
Would now outshine their dull Latin versions and cause scholars further to seek.
Yes, between the death of Wycliffe in 1384 and the advent of Luther's ninety-five theses,
The world had greatly changed, and church tradition was falling to pieces.
Following Wycliffe, both Tyndale and Luther declared only the Scripture reliable
And defied the pope by translating into their native tongues the Holy Bible.
Tyndale's New Testament translation was the first English Bible in print,
And Coverdale's complete Bible in English shortly followed it.
Their linguistic genius and art of phrasing imbued majesty into their mother tongue,
And on their wings the later King James version was able to soar to number one.
When we repeat the Lord's Prayer, these inspired linguists still prevail:
"Forgive us our trespasses" is Tyndale; "forgive us our debts" is Coverdale.
The Great Bible, a massive thing, and the Geneva Bible were next on the scene,
Authorized not by the pope but by the English king.
Henry VIII now claimed himself fully supreme in matters of both church and state;
He gave up his title as Defender of the Faith when the pope refused to cooperate
With his plan to put away his queen, who had failed to produce male heirs.
In his dual role, Henry took new wives along with the church's monasteries.

To the pope's dismay, Coverdale's Bible of 1537 became a firstling:
The first complete English Bible in print and the first authorized, be it a king.
The Vulgate was replaced by an English translation,
Thus causing the papacy intolerable consternation.
Two years later came the Great Bible, so declared because of adornment and size.
Though favored by Henry and his ministers, it found little support otherwise.
It was the Geneva Bible of 1560 that found itself without peer,
For it was the most accurate and well annotated Bible yet to appear.
There was some improvement on which any home could dote:
Legible print; division of chapter and verse; the explanatory note.
It served Shakespeare and early American settlers, including the Puritan.
Little did anyone suspect that even a greater translation was at hand.
Yes, in 1611 came the King James Authorized translation,
Which was destined to be an enduring sensation.
All the virtues of the previous translations came together in this one,
Giving it the greatest intrinsic excellence under the sun.
In style, the King James Bible had no peer
For it was guided by previous styles that approached the stratosphere.
There were Wycliffe, Tyndale, Coverdale, and the Geneva crew.
Yet the King James scholars still had plenty to do.
They perused every line, turned every phrase, and every word moved,
Looking for any possible arrangement or change that might improve.
Though the examples are manifold, let us pick one to represent all the rest:
"Come unto me all ye that labor and are laden and I will ease you"—Tyndale's best.
Putting this line to the test, the King James scholars enhanced it to the crest:
"Come unto me all ye that labor and are heavy laden, and I will give you rest."

Change was in the air, not only in England but everywhere.
Renaissance, Reformation, Gutenberg, Columbus—what a stir!
The masses were beginning to read and think and travel;
Old ideas, institutions, and traditions were beginning to unravel.
Catalyst to this phenomenal reaction stood the Bible, that one great book
That was being translated into the vernacular and placed in every nook.
It was no longer the exclusive document of the church to interpret authoritatively,
For the masses, believing "every man a priest," were enacting Luther's hyperbole.
Wycliffe's ashes had, indeed, spread "wide as the waters be";
And God's word in the vernacular was available for all to see.
The great work of the Morning Star of the Reformation was coming to fruition;
The merchant and the plowman now deciphered truth, their own rendition.
They read the Old Testament through and through
To learn what man could and could not do.
They learned about the law, which exposed man's sin,
But did not find how to be cleansed again.
Then in the New Testament, the plan of salvation was fully explained:
It was not in the doing but in the believing that grace was to be attained.
They read their Bibles, and on the Sabbath and every weekday too;
They used their Bibles to find out what everyone should do.
Whether spiritual or secular, an answer they could find.
For in their Bible they found exemplary precedents of every kind
To guide either yeoman or nobleman, who in God's eyes were the same.
Equal justice, they declared, was a God-given right, regardless of station or fame.
The English commons were reining in both the clergy and the king;
They could read and think, and they boldly held tight the purse string
When Charles I adamantly persisted in his divine-right-of-king thinking,

The commons, filled with reformed and informed Puritans, let loose their sting;
They believed their perceived truth based on Scripture, far superior to that of the king,
And declared it their duty to remove him, no matter how inauspicious this might seem.
As Puritans perceived it, they were in a covenant relationship with the Lord God,
And it was their responsibility to keep the realm pure and not to spare the rod.
Under their covenant tie to God, they were responsible for corruption in the land.
Consequently, they must, being of the elect, take a formidable stand,
As God's new-chosen Israelites, they must curb wickedness in their native England
Before God looked down and again poured out his wrath on the culprit man.
Not for a minute could they afford to stick their heads in the sand.
It was the head of Charles that must be removed to save the commonweal,
Even though the thought of commons beheading a king seemed unreal.
The deed done, commoner Oliver Cromwell stepped forward to take the lead.
He said his Roundhead saints declared themselves the ones to see to England's need.
They saw the need to bend England to the will of God.
So through all the land, the banning of iniquities they gave the nod.
From Charles' execution in 1649 until Cromwell's untimely demise in 1658,
The Puritan spirit waxed strong in England and tried to keep the country straight.
Despite this well-meaning zeal, all was not rosy in the commonweal.
Many wished for a lessening of this Puritan straightness and began to appeal.

For a while, Cavaliers held the upper hand but could not fully restrain Puritan zeal.
It took the Glorious Revolution of 1688 to forge a compromise that was real.
Though monarchy returned, commons held its ground;
William of Orange was called by Parliament, not the other way around.
And the limits to his powers were prescribed in a bill of rights:
He, and future kings, would be guided by commons' lights.
For commoners could now read the holy word, the source of truth and authority.
And truth and authority were what the majority of commoners perceived them to be.
This was true not only for England but for its New England colonies across the sea,
Where Puritans had been in charge previous to Puritan rule in the mother country.
In America, the Puritans read their Geneva Bibles very carefully, searching for direction
In every walk of life; they even prescribed a special sermon previous to each election.
One elected governor, John Winthrop, in sermon defined his colony's great mission:
To be a city upon a hill, a light to all the world—undeniably, an awesome commission.
The Puritans, following their Bible teachings, set the bar high.
And such a worthy goal newcomers could never truly deny;
Americans read the Bible in their favorite translations—: Geneva, King James, Revised—
Said their prayers, and spread out over the promised land in every guise;
They revolted from their mother country to set up a more democratic government,
Which became the United States of America, a most noble experiment,
Continuing to this present day still driven by Wycliffe-type sentiment.

Dear reader, we pray the foregoing review of a timely portion of religious history
Helps clarify the role of the Bible and the Puritans in shaping America's history.

BEN FRANKLIN'S EXEMPLARY STAND

Benjamin Franklin (1709–90): founding father, printer, writer, statesman, scientist, philosopher, diplomat, inventor, exceptional

It can be said that Ben Franklin not only invented himself
But that he also invented the secret of wealth.
To publish his inventions was always Franklin's intent,
And in so doing to change his country's bent.
His publication *Way to Wealth* became instantly stellar,
Replacing Wigglesworth's *Day of Doom* as best seller.
Calvinist theology, for a century or more, had been the beacon divine,
But now economics was beginning to climb, leaving religion behind.
Franklin rejected the sermon as the preferred method of instruction,
Believing the aphorism stimulated greater production.
He filled his annually published almanac with aphorisms galore
And let them drop from the mouth of Poor Richard as gems of folklore.
Franklin knew that the aphorism would stick in the mind
But that the sermon would often be left behind.
Believing that a simple formula would keep man from being mean,
Franklin named the essential virtues in a list of thirteen;
Of the thirteen virtues that he assiduously deified,
Industry and frugality were foremost, and together tied.
Industry was imperative for gaining;
Frugality was imperative for retaining.
Yet wealth, Franklin insisted, was not man's ultimate goal;
It simply supplied greater possibilities for the soul.
He declared that man served God by serving his fellow man,
And on that general premise, Franklin took his exemplary stand.[10]

---

10 For more about the remarkably gifted and talented Benjamin Franklin, read my book *What Makes America Great*, available online at Amazon and Barnes & Noble.

Another Look at America's Greatness

What Makes America Great (WMAG)

Author Bob Dowell, PhD

This little book (*WMAG*) addresses America's greatness,
Its case grounded in history and presented in succinctness,
Respecting the reader's preference for facts and conciseness.
The author has sifted through America's history and literature,
Searching diligently for clues abundant before any conjecture relate,
Seeking first irrefutable evidence of just what makes America great.
First, we find a belief in God, a belief shared by the secular state design,
For America was birthed by the Reformation, a fervently religious time.

Next, we see a fervently religious settler, the Puritan, to America set sail,
Believing God's call assured that against Satan's wiles they would prevail,
There declare the true gospel and build a state on principles the Bible way.
Exhibit A: witness Plymouth Plantation (Colony) and Massachusetts Bay.
Many Puritans felt they were the new Israelites chosen to reverse things appalling,
Believing the Israelites first, then the church Roman Catholic had failed their calling.
Thus, the Puritan out of the Reformation called to begin in the new world anew,
And that is what the Puritans of Plymouth and Massachusetts came here to do.
In 1620 and 1630, to America they came, led by Bradford and Winthrop, respectively,
Who left their mark indelibly: *Plymouth Plantation* and *A Model of Christian Charity*.
Winthrop declared, we have covenanted with God exemplary to be, and so we must.
Should we perjure ourselves, God will most assuredly break out in wrath against us;
We must live exemplary, we must be *as a city upon a hill* for all the world to see.
And is not the phrase *as a city upon a hill* often used in praising America presently?
Bradford filled his history *Of Plymouth Plantation* with references to *providence*;
Major occurrences, ill or good, he viewed as provident: God's covenant governance.
As America progressed from colonies to the United States, it kept its religious bent,

Not in theocratic form but in secular form, separating church and state the intent.
Churches of various denominations fill the land, promoting God's word untold,
Ministers laboring to maintain a measure of the Reformation fervency of old,
The nation's motto, In God We Trust, on its currency, bill and coin, printed bold,
The speeches of US presidents ending with a prayerful "and God Bless America,"
Our World War II soldiers repeating the adage "There are no atheists in foxholes!"
Belief is deeply embedded in our Declaration of Independence, a secular document.
Note the separation of our colonies from England justified in terms of God's consent;
Jefferson writes "that all men are created equal, that they are endowed by their Creator
With certain unalienable rights," words Martin L. King Jr. has called America's creed,
Declaring so in his "I Have a Dream" speech, beseeching America to live by its creed
Stated in its Declaration and guaranteed in its Constitution but still lacking in deed.
Martin L. King Jr. and Elizabeth C. Stanton for two major minorities campaigned:
African Americans and women, whose God-given rights were a long time restrained.
The notable contributions of this dynamic duo must be praised for success attained;
The Declaration of Sentiments and "I Have a Dream" redefined America's moral frame.
Color and gender discrimination challenged America's creed, putting it to test severe,

A test eventually passed by holding fast to belief in God, and thereby his laws revere.

There is much, much more to tell about America's greatness, all easily substantiated,

But since I do so in my book *What Makes America Great*, let this poem be terminated.

To read the story in greater detail, I invite you to view my book page on amazon.com,

Where my book family resides, each hoping to be the viewer's choice number one.

However, should you barnesandnoble.com prefer, please go to my book page there,

And there meet my blessed book family, each eager its thematic narrative to share.

Jonathan Edwards, Man of Zeal

Jonathan Edwards (1703–58): famous New England evangelical Puritan minister, theologian, and philosopher

Jonathan Edwards expended tremendous zeal
Hoping to convert everyone in the commonweal.
He sincerely believed that the end-time was near,
And for the unregenerate he held great fear
That time would overtake the reprobate,
That God's grace would be recognized too late.
So Edwards turned his zeal up another level
And preached mightily about hell and the devil.
With vivid images he described the horrors of that place
And fervently affirmed that the only escape was through God's grace.
Knowing the unregenerate ones were reluctant to hear,
Edwards sought to reach them by generating fear.
Using artful rhetoric, Edwards prepares a very scary sermon,
In which he compares the unregenerate to loathsome vermin.
He suspends these sinners just beyond hell's bane
But extends God's hand to hold them above the flame,
Even though their rejection stares raise God's ire
And inclines him to prefer them in the fire.
Warning the unregenerate ones that God's patience is wearing thin,
Edwards explains to them the theology of "now" and "then":
Now, *you* have the chance—perhaps *your* last—to awaken to God's grace,
But then,—meaning *your* death or end-time—*you're* in that burning place
Where the flames of God's wrath enwraps *you* on its floor
While *you* writhe and wail for evermore."

Now, twenty-first-century critics call Edwards' deprecating rhetoric politically incorrect.
Then, Edwards, rather than let the sinner burn, zealously tried to save his wretched neck.

Jefferson:
The Declaration
and the Exemplary

Thomas Jefferson (1743–1826): Founding Father, principal author of the Declaration of Independence, statesman, diplomat, architect, philosopher

Jefferson, being born into the planter aristocracy,
Grew up in a system that fostered hypocrisy;
He owned slaves, knowing it was wrong—
Even said so, and still went along.
Yet he sowed the seeds for the problem's resolution,
Even if he could not offer an immediate solution.
Jefferson, a man of genius and ingenuity,
Did great things for his beloved country.
The Louisiana Purchase immensely increased our size.
But the Declaration is undoubtedly our greatest prize.
The composition of this incomparable document
Fostered the world's greatest governmental experiment.
Jefferson's immortal words "that all men are created equal"
Have neither prequel nor sequel,
Even though he called it self-evident and true—
Along with the Continental Congress too.
It was a phrase that resonated around the globe;
For humanity, it was a treasure trove.
It catapulted democracy to a major player in world history.
It fed the main currents of America's developing destiny.
For it codified its most lofty characteristic: *the exemplary.*

The Declaration declared not only equality but also inalienable rights, no less,
Declared inalienable the rights to "life, liberty, and the pursuit of happiness."
For they came from the highest authority: "the God of nature and nature's laws."
They were for elevating the human community despite the community's flaws.
To protect these inalienable rights, a government must exist.
And it must be understood that its purpose for being is simply this.
Further understood, its power is vested in the people who elect it—
And if that it fails to serve its purpose, to get rid of it is legitimate.
No doubt, Jefferson's Declaration is a milestone in the world's long history,
And in the realm of government and equality, it remains *the most exemplary*.

The Sacrament of Communion

Whether called Communion, Eucharist, Lord's Supper, or Mass,
It's one holy sacrament that all Christians hold fast.
The blessing of the bread, the blessing of the wine
Begins this sacrament celebrating the sacrifice of Jesus Christ divine.
The minister or the priest prays for consecration;
The laity prays for remission and contrition.
Whether the view is transubstantiation, consubstantiation, or symbol,
Preparation for partaking may make the sinner tremble.
It is well known that Paul reminded the Corinthians the need for self-examination,
For partaking in a flippant manner, he warned, would be cause for damnation.
Whether the elements are viewed as symbol or divine,
At the moment of intake they become more than bread or wine.
At the moment of intake, the recipient sinner becomes a holy temple.
Through cleansing prayer and confession focused on the pure and simple,
Shriven of ill will and contention, and the heart in its proper place,
The sinner is prepared for taking in the elements, thereby taking in God's grace.
Some congregations celebrate this sacrament more frequently than others.
Even so, they remain ecumenical Christian sisters and brothers.
Catholic, Orthodox, or Protestant can find no exact biblical prescription,
So congregations rely on enlightened preference and long-standing tradition.
Whatever the frequency of celebration, on one point all Christians can agree:

That Christ did say, "As oft as ye do it, do it in remembrance of me."
Whether the elements miraculously become his flesh and blood (transubstantiation)
Or whether His presence mysteriously accompanies the elements (consubstantiation)
Or whether the elements remain bread and wine but sacred symbols,
It is the sacrament that reminds sinners of their eternal need of grace;
It is the sacrament that sustains them till they meet their Savior face-to-face.

Walking with Mary: In Nazareth, in Bethlehem, in Jerusalem

This preface and poem were written after having visited the Holy Land with a church group.

Many thoughts flood one's mind when visiting the Holy Land, especially so if it's the first time. I realized this last February (2010) as my wife, Nancy, and I toured the Holy Land with a church group. When we stopped at a particular location marking the spot where a major biblical event is believed to have occurred, many thoughts entered my mind as I listened to our tour guide and then recalled the Bible narrative describing the event. One of those stops lingered in my mind after returning home from the Holy Land, compelling me to reflect further on the event. The place is Nazareth, and the event is the Annunciation, Gabriel's announcing to Mary that she has been chosen to birth the Son of God!

I tried to imagine how this teenage maid must have felt having an angel appear and announce to her that she was about to become the mother of the Son of God. A startling revelation! And further startling: the teenage maid was already spoken for! She was betrothed (engaged) to a man named Joseph and now told she is to have the Son of God. Indeed, a startling revelation!

It took a great deal of faith and courage for the young betrothed maid to process the announcement, the revelation. Even though the angel Gabriel assures her, she still needs human support and assurance. But where can she turn? Not to Joseph! Not to her mother! She needs a confidant. And Gabriel has given her the clue by telling Mary that her relative Elizabeth is six months pregnant with a divinely announced child. (We know, because Luke has told us, that this same Gabriel had earlier appeared to Zacharias, a priest and husband to Elizabeth, and told him that even though he is aged and Elizabeth is barren and also aged, it is God's will they have a son; and behold, Elizabeth does become pregnant and does go into seclusion.) Just how much of this Mary knows, we cannot know, but as soon as Gabriel departs, she thinks of Elizabeth. How do we know this? Luke says, "And Mary arose and went into the hill country with <u>haste</u>."[11] She sets out on an eighty-mile journey to Ein Kerem, the home of Elizabeth and Zacharias. Apparently, Mary and Elizabeth were close, Elizabeth to Mary like a mentor "big sister," for Elizabeth is obviously much older than is Mary.

Now that I've set the stage, please allow me to proceed with my reflections conceptualized in the form of a poem. You know, the early visitors to the Holy Land could build shrines at designated spots where major biblical events happened. And Constantine's mother, St. Helena, one of those early visitors who, with the blessings of her emperor son, had a stone-and-mortar shrine built in Bethlehem over the place where Jesus was born. But later visitors, like us, to the Holy Land, seeing the stone-and-mortar shrines, long ago established, are only left with the option of building a shrine of words, so the following poem is my word shrine for the Annunciation.

Walking with Mary in Nazareth, in Bethlehem, in Jerusalem,
Imagine a time almost ending BC, but before it was known as BC,
And a hill country village of no consequence in a region called Galilee,
A village named Nazareth and the home of a betrothed maid named Mary,
Betrothed to a man named Joseph, betrothed and in a year or so to wed,
Dutifully the young virgin thinks toward adulthood and the marriage bed.
Marriage and children made a maid's life complete, so Holy Scripture said.
Now, imagine the young maid's surprise when an angel appears ever near,

---

11 Luke 1:39.

Fearful she has to be with a divine being standing there with message clear;
"Rejoice highly favored one, blessed are you among women, chosen maid,"[12]
But in Scriptural tradition, the angel Gabriel was quick to say, "Be not afraid,"[13]
Surely reassuring to the startled maid, visibly stunned by this awesome event,
Yet fear fades to puzzlement as angel Gabriel continues with announcement:
"Mary, having found favor with God, you will, in your womb, conceive thus,
And in time you shall bring forth a Son, and you shall call his name Jesus,
And he will be great and will be called the Son of the Most High above,
And the Lord above will give him the throne of David, his Father's beloved,
And he shall reign over the house of Jacob for all time to come,
And of His kingdom there shall be no end for all time to come."[14]
Puzzled, Mary asks how this birth can be since no man has she known.
The angel tells her the Holy Spirit will come to you, Mary, chosen one,
And overshadow you, and the Holy One born will be the Son of God.
Thus, of all the maids of the world, to Mary goes the Most High's nod.
Also, her relative Elizabeth has conceived through divine intervention;
Though aged and barren, she is six months with child, God's intention.
"Know that with God nothing is impossible,"[15] the angel is quick to opine,
Thereby furnishing Mary further assurance that what she hears is divine;
Reassured by angel and spirit, Mary responds obediently from the heart,

---

12 Luke 1:28.
13 Luke 1:30.
14 Luke 1:31–33.
15 Luke 1:37.

"Let it be to me according to your word,"[16] as Gabriel prepares to depart;
Alone, the young maid senses solace as her thoughts to Elizabeth turn,
To one six months within miraculous conception, from this elder learn.
"Then Mary arose," Luke informs us, "and went into the hill country with haste";[17]
There to a city of Judea, the house of Zacharias, to see Elizabeth face-to-face,
And when Mary greeted Elizabeth, the baby in Elizabeth's womb leaped.
Elizabeth, filled with the Holy Spirit and guided thereby, began to speak:
"Blessed are you among women, and blessed is the fruit of your womb;
But why has the Spirit granted that the mother of my Lord to me come?"[18]
It is a question rhetorical, for Elizabeth answers her own query, speaking sublime,
And what she says is Spirit tailored to confirm for young Mary her calling divine:
"The babe in my womb leaped with joy the moment your greeting sounded in my ears.
Blessed are you who believed, for fulfillment will come as sure as come the years."[19]
This confirmation was what Mary had sought from relative Elizabeth, wife of a priest,
Wife whose childbearing years were barren, but now through God's will comes feast.
After angel message confirmed by relative revered, Mary voices praise pure:

---

16 Luke 1:38.
17 Luke 1:39.
18 Luke 1:42–43.
19 Luke 1:41.

"My soul magnifies the Lord, and my spirit rejoices in God my Savior sure,[20]
Who exalted the lowly status of his maidservant that blessed she shall be called,
Great things the mighty one has done; of those who fear him, mercy falls on all.
The strength of his strong arm scatters the proud, thus thrones of the mighty fall;
He exalts the lowly, fills the hungry; his mercy dwells on those who fear him: all.
He has helped his servant Israel in remembrance of his promise to our fathers,
To Abraham, and to his seed forever," says Mary, heart and spirit led, informing others.
Like Hannah of old, Mary praises the Lord who mercifully blesses the meek and lowly.
Mary's song of praise reveals her steadfast faith and her cognizance of Scripture holy.
Her praise will become canticle called the Magnificat, a hymn universally sung.
Thus, devout maid Mary was called by God to bear his Son, the Savior soon to come.
Three months Mary stayed with Elizabeth, possibly witnessing the birth of John—
The latter conjecture, for Luke mentions Mary no more till time for her child to come.
Meanwhile, Zacharias and Elizabeth and the advent of son John take center stage.
Several months later, it is Mary again taking center stage, the event that ends an age:
Caesar Augustus decree "that all the world should be registered" reached Nazareth.

---

20 Here begins the Magnificat, Mary's response to Gabriel's announcement that she would give birth to God's Son, Jesus Christ. (See Luke 1:46–55.)

All were to go to their own city to be registered, so Joseph and Mary set
our forthwith.
Because Joseph was of the lineage of David, his own city would be that
of Bethlehem.
Though heavy with child, Mary travels with Joseph there for officials to
register them.
It so happened that upon entering Bethlehem, Mary's days were
complete for delivery,
And "she brought forth her firstborn Son," the event later to be known
as the Nativity.
She brought him forth, "wrapped him in swaddling cloth and in a
manger laid him
For there was no room at the inn,"[21] only the lowly stable
accommodations for them.
That this birth occurred in a Bethlehem stable was, of course, a
providential thing:
Micah had prophesied that out of tiny Bethlehem would come the
everlasting king.
Yet Israel envisioned Messiah a conquering king coming to crush their
foe,
Not a babe wrapped in swaddling cloth lying in a manger where
shepherds go;
But as God would have it, his Son would be lowly born at this prescribed
sight,
And in nearby fields shepherds would be keeping watch over their flocks
by night.
An angel stood before them, and the glory of God shone down like
burnished gold;
Seeing the shepherds sorely afraid, the angel tells them to be not afraid,
and behold!
Behold, I bring good tidings of great joy, tidings for all people, tidings
for accord.

---

21   Luke 2:7.

"There is born to you this day, in the city of David a Savior who is Christ the Lord.
This will be a sign to you, a babe wrapped in swaddling clothes lying in a manger."[22]
Imagine the awe these shepherds felt hearing the words of this divine stranger!
Not to mention the multitude of heavenly host who descend praising God, then
Saying, "Glory to God in the highest, and on earth peace, goodwill toward men."[23]
Message delivered, angel and heavenly host ascend skyward while shepherds mass
And reverently say, "Let us go to Bethlehem and see this thing that has come to pass.
This thing that God has made known to us," and thus in haste the shepherds set off
To find Mary, Joseph, and, in a manger, the "babe wrapped in swaddling cloth."[24]
There in the stable, as the angels said, lay the Babe, the Savior born, Christ the Lord.
After seeing him, the shepherds witnessed widely this divine event, all in accord.
And all who heard them marveled at these things the shepherds passed on to them,
"But Mary kept all these things and pondered them in her heart"[25] while adoring him
And harking back to the angel Gabriel's visit when, as virgin maid betrothed, she
Heard the angel say, "Rejoice, favored one," chosen maid, mother of God's Son to be.

---

22 Luke 2:11–12.
23 Luke 2:13.
24 Luke 2:16.
25 Luke 2:19.

Then the shepherds return to the fields praising God, their lives never to be the same.
Eight days later the manger child is circumcised and called Jesus, his designated name.
It is the name given by the angel Gabriel when informing Mary she his mother to be.
Now Mary is mother and has much to ponder as many seek out the child Jesus to see:
First the shepherds seek him out as the angel instructed them on that midnight clear,
And during the trip to the temple, from Simeon and Anna more praise Mary will hear.
What does the story of the Annunciation and Nativity when told today mean to you and me?
In our minds do we not walk with Mary and Joseph to Bethlehem, there the lowly manger to see?
Like the shepherds, do we not visit this scene to view the babe wrapped in swaddling cloth?
Surely we do, for Luke's story rings in our ears signaling the Holy Spirit to lift our hearts aloft.
Surely at each yuletide, we walk with Mary and Joseph to Bethlehem, there renewing our accord,
Thus again attuning our spirits to God's Spirit that the Christ child vision confirms to us our Lord.

Gideon Then and Now

Gideon's story is told in the book of Judges, chapters 6–8.

The Old Testament Gideon lives on in the modern world today.
How could such a miraculous thing be, you may say?
It's a story almost incredible, as was the original in Judges told,
The book of the Bible in which several incredible stories unfold,
Chronicling major events between Joshua's death and the monarchy,
Events in which the Israelites angered God because of their apostasy.
When the Israelites practiced apostasy, God punished them:
Given into the hand of their enemy and thereby condemned,
Allowed to suffer relentlessly until they cried out repentantly;
Then God would designate one to fill with spirit abundantly,
So a sovereign judge he could be to defeat the dreaded enemy
And lead his people back to the Lord and away from apostasy.
God called Gideon the judge to be when Midian was the enemy.
Midianites, like locusts, came destroying the Israelite economy.
The angel of the Lord greeted Gideon, calling him a mighty warrior,
A greeting Gideon challenged, saying his Manasseh clan was inferior,
Being the weakest one of all and he the least among his family.
No doubt his challenge is combination of both fear and humility.
"Nevertheless," responds the angel, "the Lord is with you absolutely!"
"How can that be," asks Gideon, "when we are violated mercilessly?
Surely the Lord has abandoned us, for Midian plunders our land."
"Hear," says the Lord, "I will be with you, and you will dispel Midian."
Wanting to make sure it was God directing him, Gideon asks for time
Time to prepare an offering, one that would please the Lord divine.
The offering prepared, God's angel tells him, "On this rock lay it."
The angel touches it with the tip of his staff, and fire consumes it.
At that moment the angel disappears, prompting Gideon to say,

"Now I know for sure it was God's angel who visited me this day."
Thus, it is imperative Gideon build an altar the Lord God to revere.
No sooner done than Gideon hears God's voice sounding in his ear,
Saying, "Tear down your father's baal altar and build a proper one."
In the dark of the night, Gideon works feverishly to get the job done,
For fear of his family and the men of the town, baal worshippers all.
Daylight revealing what Gideon had done, his father Joash gets a call.
The townsmen demand that Joash give up his son to be punished anon,
For he has torn down the altar of baal and replaced it with another one.
Joash, defending his son, says, "If Baal truly is a god he can himself defend,
Why should you plead baal's case? Why think it your duty baal to defend?
Then, they called Gideon "Jerub-Baal," meaning "Let baal with him contend."
The baal issue faded as hordes of Midianites like locusts swarmed their land.
And Gideon, filled with the Spirit of the Lord, immediately took command,
Calling on the Israelite tribes to join him in defending their promised land.
Though visited by God's angel and God's Spirit received, Gideon asks more.
"Again assure, me Lord, if by my hand you will save Israel from Median hoard
If I place a fleece on the threshing floor and it collects dew and the ground none;
Then I shall know that you are still with me and will not fear the battle to come."
The next day Gideon squeezes a bowl of water from the fleece onto ground dry.
Surely God has answered me in the affirmative, but one more sign I wish to try.

"Please do not be angry, Lord, if I ask just one more sign for confidence anew:
If tomorrow the fleece is dry and the ground wet with dew, I'll know it's you."
When morning revealed fleece dry and ground wet, Gideon's faith soared.
Reassured, he and his thirty-two thousand men camp at the spring of Harod
To work out their strategy for combat against the numerous Midian force,
But God has his own plan and informs Gideon to reduce his Israelite force.
So that Israel may not boast that her own strength has saved her from harm,
Gideon is informed to significantly reduce the number of his Israelites armed.
Any armed Israelite who trembles with fear must immediately leave for home.
A recounting of the Israelite force revealed that twenty-two thousand had gone.
Though ten thousand being left, God informs Gideon still more need to exit.
A second test needed to reduce numbers: observe the men's drinking habit.
Most of the ten thousand kneeled at the water's edge and drank facedown,
But three hundred men lifted water to their mouth in order to look around.
God tells Gideon with the three hundred "I will give Midian into your hands."
Leaving their provisions and trumpets, all the others returned to their lands.
Below the Israelite camp was the Midianite camp, numerous as a locust swarm.

God knew Gideon and the three hundred specially chosen might be alarmed.
So he awakens Gideon and sends him on a spy mission behind the enemy line,
Telling him to stealthy stalk the Median camp and sample their state of mind.
Arriving, Gideon hears a Midian soldier telling another his troubling dream:
"A loaf of barley bread came rolling into our camp, demolishing everything!"
"That can mean only one thing, my friend, the sword of Gideon upon us lands;
God favors Israelites, Gideon led, and will give us Midianites into his hands."
Hearing the dream interpretation, Gideon to his sleeping camp ran
And called out, "Get up, the Lord has given the Midianites into your hand."
The three hundred divide into three groups, each with torch and empty jar.
Thus, three companies of one hundred men each are now equipped for war.
A torch inside the jar in one hand and a trumpet in the other, they all set out,
Prepared on signal to smash jars, hold up torches, blow trumpets, and shout.
Gideon instructs three companies, saying, "Follow me, and do exactly as I do."
Trumpets blare, torches flare, and all shout, "A sword for the Lord, and Gideon too"
When the three hundred reach the edge of the Median camp, deep in slumber.
Awakened startled and frightened, the Midianites fled tents in record number.

Panic-stricken they fled, swords drawn, inadvertently slaughtering one another.
Engulfed in darkness and chaos, they could not distinguish whether foe or brother.
God guided Gideon and the three hundred in routing a hundred thousand plus
Who without doubt thought to themselves, "The honor belongs to God, not to us."
The thousands of Midianites surviving the midnight rout continued to flee in haste,
But the Israelite tribes Naphtali and Asher and Manasseh joined Gideon in the chase,
And Israelites from the tribe Ephraim raced to the Jordan to secure the river's fords.
Buoyed by Gideon's rout, the Israelites come en masse eager to wield their swords.
The Midianite oppressors destroyed, the Israelites asked Gideon to rule over them,
But Gideon wisely replies, "I will not rule over you; God is our ruler, and only him."
Thus Gideon learned what the Israelites had to learn over and over, times untold.
The book of Judges records this lesson so painfully learned by the Israelites of old.
And reading the book of Judges surely reminds us that the lesson is a recurring one
Each generation must learn and parents must pass on lest their children be undone.
Gideon demonstrated the lesson well, and his spiritual children, Gideons International,
Not only learn the lesson well also but in the role of parent pass it on exceedingly well.
Hotel and motel rooms worldwide house a Gideon Bible for guest accommodation;

Many a testimony praises the Gideon Bible for its role in their search for salvation.

As Gideon learned and told his people, God must rule if you desire a life of peace,

Was this not wisdom plus? Where God rules not, secular tyranny will never cease?

Whether *then*, when Gideon lived, or *now*, when his namesake lives, the need remains;

So let us thank the Lord for Gideon *then* and his namesake *now* for taking the reins.

My Unforgettable Bird Dogs Lou and Ike

Though these two incredible hunting partners passed years ago, they are very much alive in my memories.

Dr. Bob and his bird dogs

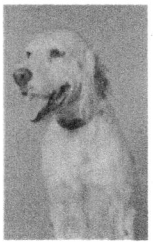

Lou Ike

When I think of my late hunting partner Lou,
The emotions that well up are always two:
One of sadness followed by one of joy.
Sadness comes first, the feeling of loss;
Then joy arrives the sadness to toss.

For memory recalls well-trained Lou very much alive
And eager to perform the thing on which she thrived,
Quartering the ag land to and fro for a whiff of just one scent,
That of the elusive quail, and scenting where the covey went,
So far doing mostly instinctively what a bird dog is bred to do—
But finding the covey without flushing it, mostly the trained Lou.
I never tired of watching Lou expertly working a covey of quail;
It was always a captivating sight, a show without aesthetic equal.
She knew the exact distance to slow pursuit and to stealthy advance,
Knew when the quail had stopped and assumed a freeze as if in a trance,
Presuming their chosen cover and stillness would their pursuer deceive;
But Lou was never deceived, for by sight and by scent she could perceive.
Yet whether the quail remained in frozen mode or burst into panic flight
Depended on Lou sizing up the situation and then doing everything right;
At just the proper distance, she, too, must go into frozen mode, body stiff,
Tail raised and rigid, head high and level, right front leg in slight uplift.
That's my signal to advance, my sweet sixteen in hand and covey flush,
While Lou watches, waiting for a bird to fold and fall to retrieve for us.
The quail hunter code I greatly respected and kept in mind:
Never leave a wounded bird behind; search until you find.
Lou and I must have walked a million miles pursuing our obsession;
She was always waiting eagerly for the next quail-hunting session.
When finishing my PhD and settling in at ETSU, we make room for Lou;
After viewing the extensive ETSU ag land, I knew it was the thing to do.
Teaching, research, and committees, the big three academic chores, bred stress,
But what mattered stress when Lou stood ready to provide the perfect redress?
Frequently, Lou and I set out to roam the ETSU ag land in search of the wily quail;

Miles upon miles I happily followed tireless Lou searching for a quail-scented trail.
Of course, our out-of-season hunts were limited to exercise and training only,
So we added puppy Ike to intensify training and to keep Lou from being lonely.
Little Ike, innately talented, progressed with lightning speed;
Watching him perform at six months old was a sight indeed.
The little fellow was sometimes sightless lunging through weeds tall,
But no matter how rugged the terrain, little Ike negotiated it all.
Neither a fleeing rabbit nor a flushed meadowlark distracted concentration;
He stayed focused on detecting the scent of the wily quail's current location.
Lou and Ike were always eager to take the field, regardless of the weather
Each respected the other, no jealousy shown; they loved hunting together.
How blessed to be: incomparable bird dogs and hunt time set aside,
But one major irony I could not abide no matter how much I tried:
The quail population in East Texas was in serious decline;
Every year finding a covey of quail required more time.
Solving the problem would require a move; that was plain to see.
I thought I knew the perfect place but must first consider the family.
The place in mind was near the Rio Grande, where two cultures blend,
And common sense says that such an environment would education amend,
And surveys say that dry lands near the Rio Grande numerous quail maintain.
And, I say, would not providing talented Lou and Ike prolific terrain be humane?
My greatest regret is that Lou passed before the move completed.
Otherwise, the move proved even better than contemplated.

Ike and I thrived hunting the wily quail so abundant near the Rio Grande;
The family became bilingual to more readily blend and understand.
But to this day, decades later, I still think of my superb hunting partner Lou
And shed a tear or two; then Ike comes to mind, conjuring a few tears too.
But joy prevails when memory conjures images of Lou and Ike on scented trail,
Together performing a flawless demonstration on how to work the wily quail.

Nanny and Papa Meet Allison

Papa addresses the guests at his grandson Will's rehearsal dinner party.

When Nanny and Papa heard our grandson Will had a special girlfriend,
We looked at each other and said in unison, "Wonder if her family is Texan?"
Then we learned, yes, she's from Dallas and belongs to the Turpin clan.
Nanny and I were getting pretty excited, thinking, this is grand.
Then it occurred to us, but we haven't even met this young lady yet;
Our excitement turned to anxiety, eliciting tiny beads of sweat.
Yes, a meeting needs to take place and needs to take place soon;
Out came cell phones exploring possibilities well into the afternoon.
Why not a meeting at what we facetiously call the family farm palace,
Our double-wide in the pasture? Location: eighty miles east of Dallas.
Will and Allison graciously consented to meet us at our pastoral retreat,
Half hidden behind forest and fence line, far from any city or paved street.
The young and the old, the present and the past, perhaps a new beginning,
Perhaps parents and grandparents soon to see their Texas branches extending—
Thus contemplating, Nanny and Papa stood out on the farmhouse deck waiting,
Waiting and thinking while anxiety worked tireless, leaving us a little uptight
Until Allison alighted, lovely and gracious and unassuming: it was love at first sight!
It had to be a God thing, for it was truly awesome.
We already knew our Will to be the paragon:
Our handsome, loving, gracious Christian grandson.

Now we see him teamed with feminine equal, Allison.
Fast-forward and here we are tonight, Dowells and Turpins, extended families and friends,
Here to toast Allison and Will and wish them well, for tomorrow their marriage begins.
Are we not here tonight to wish this couple the best in the days to come?
And are we not committed to doing so graciously, each and every one?
May our pledge be "Humor we embrace, but crudity we deplore"?
May it be on the wings of graciousness that we soar?
Lest I become pedantic, I shall now sit down and say no more!

Santa's Christmas Gift Story

Santa's here.

A tradition at the Dowell family is Papa (grandfather) playing Santa on Christmas Eve. He always has a special gift for the children (now adults) and grandchildren, which he introduces by reading an instructive poem related to the gift.

Children and grandchildren, lend Santa your ear;
There's a history lesson he wants you to hear.
It's a lesson about our founding fathers, all first-rate!
Their blessed vision and how it made America great.
The full details I will later cover in a full-length book,
But for now we will simply take a brief look.
To heaven, first priority, they unanimously gave,
For life, they all knew, extends beyond the grave.
Else why did our Creator us a manual give,
The Bible, to prepare us for an afterlife to live?
To foster earthly prosperity was their second priority;
Industry and frugality they declared an absolute necessity.
Worship and work they gave the highest priority,
Declaring these two virtues the most exemplary.

Wisely they extolled them, thereby keeping the colonists on track.
That they did so I wish to substantiate through indisputable fact.
From 1662 to 1757, a religious book, *The Day of Doom*, topped the best seller list
For a century; this poetical description of the Last Judgment trumped all the rest.
Then, in 1758, Franklin's *The Way to Wealth* catapulted into first place.
Though it moved into first place, it did not *The Day of Doom* replace.
Side by side, the theological and the economic stood,
Expounding both the spiritual and the secular virtues good.
The perceptive Franklin knew the two were inextricably intertwined.
Allow me to explicate his wise thinking by paraphrasing it in poetic line.
Do not, he cautions, depend exclusively on your own industry and frugality—
Though, unquestionably, exemplary virtues, they may at any time blasted be
Without the blessing of heaven humbly received.
Therefore, seek that blessing: be not self-deceived.
Enough of my telling you about our country's founders great
And their outstanding and best-selling books, all first-rate.
I want you to read them on your own so you can truly understand
Why and how the country you live in is the planet's promised land.
So Ben Franklin's *The Way to Wealth* is on its way,
But lo, it will not arrive before Christmas day.
Consequently, to assuage our disappointment sore,
We shopped frantically for something else you might adore.
Fortunately, we found something we think will delight,
So please open it,[26] and tell us if we're right!

---

[26] Each was handed an envelope containing one Franklin bill (US currency) and a note saying, "Amazon is delivering *The Way of Wealth* to you." Yes, everyone was delighted!

Meditation on Brenda's Birthday Fifty

Adoration of baby Brenda

Lo! Surely half a century has not come and gone
Since blessed baby Brenda first graced our home,
Bringing great joy to her mom and dad and brothers too!
In the hovering presence of parents and siblings, you grew.
The lack of constant adoration you seldom ever knew
Dad, Mom, or brother always vying to indulge you.
Graciously, you did not allow the adoration your head swell.
Commendably, you processed it and passed it on quite well
To husband, son, and daughters as loving wife and mom,
Thereby raising a gracious loving family second to none.
All the while, time's winged chariot has moved on oh so swiftly,
And blessed baby Brenda has become blessed mom Brenda and fifty.
But let's not count the years; instead let's celebrate the blessings:
What matter years when you're blessed by family, friends, and God above?
What matter years when you're healthy, happy, and basking in enduring love?

To Colton James on His Eighteenth Birthday

A birthday note encouraging my grandson to stay focused and keep his exemplary footing as he turns eighteen and begins college.

Congratulations, Colton James, you're now eighteen,
And a fine young man, exemplary in every good thing.
Your reputation swells family pride,
So keep pacing at this excellent stride.
From high school to college, the next big step,
And Texas A&M has always been your prep.
Happily you have your invitation to Aggie Land,
Sacred institution revered by the Henderson clan.
All well and good, if you keep the right pace
And don't let the extra curricula turn your face.
Stay focused on the curricula first and foremost;
Never ever lose sight of the academic goalpost.
Otherwise you lose the necessary means
To achieve those long-cherished dreams.
You lose the education, the degree, and the renown;
You lose the essentials in which successes abound.
Keep in mind that successful hotel and angler's paradise—
The DECA[27] model you designed and modeled, oh so nice,

The kind of exemplary business model that makes America great.
So keep focused; keep your exemplary stride; keep America great!

---

27 An international organization that through real-life business scenarios prepares high school and college students to be leaders in marketing, finance, and management.

To My Grandson Colton on His Nineteenth Birthday

A birthday note commending my grandson for his exemplary extracurricular activity.

So good to hear that you're involved in spiritual activity;
Life without worship is not the way life was meant to be.
Only the Creator has understanding infinite;
The created have understanding solely finite.
We, the created, must look to the Creator for direction;
Doing otherwise would be the epitome of indiscretion.
If I may to you a suggestion give
About how life might best be lived,
Allow me to quote a line from the apostle Paul,
A verse from Philippians (4:13) that says it all:
"I can do all things through Christ who strengthens me."
And on that note, my grandson, I pray with me you agree.

Happy Mother's Day to My Wife

Happy Mother's Day, my dearest Nancy Kathleen;
For more than sixty years, you a mother have been.
Who can deny that recognition day you much deserve?
To say you do not such a day deserve, who has the nerve?
I trust a little appreciative recognition will give you a lift,
Especially so if to the verbal appreciation is added a gift.
What the appropriate gift should be, I was first at loss,
Until I thought I heard a voice say gift her a necklace cross.
Of course, a cross, most appropriate for a mother of sixty years;
Think of the inevitable agonies, large and small, all the tears.
And though the agonies of motherhood may many be,
The loving mother never thinks of them as adversity.
Sacrificing for her children, no greater joy can a mother attain;
Designate it paradox of the cross, where seeming loss is but gain.
So when you wear this little necklace cross, think of the verses above,
And rejoice in the paradox of the cross, the paradox of redeeming love.

The Story of Mighty Enron

These lines were written after reviewing my rollover IRA and noting a listing of worthless Enron stock.

Sing, O corporate muse, tell the intriguing story of once-mighty Enron,
Who analysts and investors swore was to be Wall Street's number one,
Never dreaming they would someday wish to bite their prophetic tongue.
The company was led by a charming CEO respectfully known as Mr. Ken Lay.
It seemed that whoever and whatever he touched bent his way;
He charmed the lowest employee as readily as the famous celebrity.
In Washington, DC, this Texas charmer was quite a whiz on the hill,
Dropping dandy donations in politicians' coffers, creating a fizz of goodwill.
He abided by one rule he considered golden:
"Make every politician to you beholden."
Though Mr. Ken Lay was sharp as a tack,
There was one crucial thing he lacked.
He was unaware of that old paradox:
"Sometimes the fox outfoxes the fox."
But that old paradox is a tough one to learn;
Very few learn it without a severe burn.
So Mr. Ken Lay went speedily on his way,
Wheeling and dealing, day after day,
All the while assembling a creative crew,
And thereby Enron's fame grew and grew.
He and associates were very creative too;
They could hide debt like no one else could do;
A few hundred million here and a few hundred million there,

But when Anderson auditors looked, the cupboard was bare.
And before they could say Jack Sprat,
Mr. Ken Lay was back at bat.
Hitting home runs over the fence,
Looking for more people to convince
That Enron was the company supreme,
That Enron was the investor's dream,
Having fused bricks and mortar with the internet,
Thereby making the company a Wall Street pet.
Yes, in the new economy Enron seemed a sure bet.
Employees did not worry about their 401(k);
They left its management to Mr. Ken Lay,
For they listened to what he would always say:
"Your investment fund will grow with mighty Enron,
And when you retire, you'll be worth a fortune."
Then came the shattering news
That mighty Enron was only a ruse.
Mr. Ken Lay had been so wrong;
Enron stock was hardly worth a song.
Employee's jobs and investors' funds were gone,
The exact reason being mysteriously unknown.
There was no handwriting on the wall
Explaining why mighty Enron must fall.
Blame the new economy; blame the bad economy;
Blame Mr. Ken Lay and his creative crew
For selling out early, leaving employees and investors to stew,
Leaving Washington, DC, politicians panicked over what to do.

BIDDING 2001 ADIEU

Reviewing the first year of the twenty-first century

Old 2001, we wish to bid you adieu
Before we hail 2002.
What a memorable year you have been!
So many, we cannot remember everything.
But several have left an indelible sting.
First, there was that close election between Bush and Gore,
Taking weeks for voters to find out the score.
We knew that the scorekeepers could be Congress or the Electoral College;
That the Supreme Court could decide the tally, we had no knowledge.
Of course, there was a great outcry; some were really mad.
But most were thankful to be delivered from the hanging chad.
Then the new consortium investigated thoroughly and said
It was clear that *if* Mr. Gore had not won, *then* Mr. Bush had.
Though Mr. Bush took the oath of office at the inauguration,
Mr. Clinton hung around as if he still governed the nation.
He and Hillary and staff were really reluctant to go;
It is reported that with them they took many a memento.
Poor Mr. Gore didn't have a clue what was in store for him;
It looked as though he and Tipper were way out on a limb.
Who can know what will happen to them?
But what happened to one newsmaker we do know,
That surly culprit who brought us so much woe,
Our homegrown terrorist Timothy McVeigh,
Who embraced his execution, defiant all the way.
His victims' loved ones, and other citizens, must feel some relief
That justice has silenced this misfit of terrorist belief.

Even though Clinton was squared away in his Harlem high-rise,
Washington again sprang on the country a scandalous surprise.
Intern Chandra Ann Levy, possibly a siren misfit,
Turned on married congressman Gary Condit,
Who stealthily pursued her, seeking perverted pleasures,
Until her death forced him to take different measures.
Very little would he ever reveal to the press,
But it didn't take a pundit to recognize a sordid mess.
Even the Clinton-Lewinsky scandal paled in light of this affair;
Suspicion and accusations spread everywhere.
There were constant reports broadcast on the air,
Making it abundantly clear that someone was a liar,
And constant coverage drove the public to despair.
No telling how long this sordid soap would have run
Had not al-Qaeda terrorists hit us on 911.
We saw the World Trade Center go up in flame and smoke,
And then the Pentagon severely damaged by a third strike.
TV channels spewed our news and images galore,
While shocked viewers anxiously watched, fearing more.
The days and weeks ahead furnished images varied,
Of destruction and debris, of victim famous harried.
New York revealed characteristics beyond belief;
It seemed transformed by its ordeal of grief.
Its courageous firefighters the world wanted to know;
Mayor Giuliani moved into action, soaring from zero to hero.
Nine one one virtually blotted out other major events;
Certain catastrophes, big otherwise, hardly made dents.
Almost forgotten is the Texas prison escape of seven jerks,
Who mowed down a policeman while grabbing a few perks,
And the American sub surfacing under a Japanese fishing boat,
Killing nine and sinking the boat but leaving many questions afloat.
The Chinese gunned and grounded our Navy spy plane,
Causing the US some anxiety before all again was sane.
Denise Rich defended Clinton's pardon of her billionaire ex-husband,

Claiming that neither her friend Bill nor husband made a single demand;
The media uncovered a dark spot on the Jesse Jackson rainbow coalition;
A well-paid female aide added an illegitimate daughter to the reverend's mission.
And the pitiful Andrea Yates drowns her five little ones,
Shocking the nation and stupefying its moms.
Amid all this, scientists completed the mapping of the human genome,
Giving us hope that by identifying the work of gene and chromosome,
The causes of numerous illnesses now unknown can someday be known
And the human race can look forward to a somewhat better home.
Despite such a probable physical panacea, let us not forget our fallen state;
It is the metaphysical dimension that primarily seals our fate.
Witness the resounding impact of the tragic 911,
When the physical weighed almost none and the spiritual weighed a ton.
Prayers and expressions of love were the things that mattered most.
"God bless America," we shouted from coast to coast.
Tonight, we stand fast at our post waiting for 2002,
Ready to bid old 2001 adieu,
Looking forward to the new,
Knowing that we live in an imperfect world
But praying that somehow blessings will unfurl
As we first hail, and then travel through, 2002.

Grandkids Can Teachers and Healers Be

Macy's volleyball team

For sure, grandkids can certainly teachers be;
Such are our granddaughters Lori and Macy.
Nanny and I knew zero about the game of volleyball—
OK, so we knew ball and net needed, but that's about all.
Then, high school freshman Macy made the volleyball team.
Great, but why the different-colored jersey? What does it mean?
"Why, Papa, that means I'm the libero; do not fret,"
She replies. "I return the ball when it's below the net."
Though a rational answer, I did not quite comprehend,
As Macy recognizes, and rushes her statement to amend.
"Papa, I promise to put together a little booklet thin,
With the rotating team positions, the why and when."
"And a photo roster with names," Lori chimes in.
Junior high Lori was learning the game in club Venom,

The highly touted Valley volleyball sports organization
Producing players attracting notice across the nation
And furnishing volleyball fans a double portion of enjoyment.
When the school sport season closed, to club Venom we went.
From freshman year through senior year, we followed granddaughter Macy's play,
At times offering a bit of sideline coaching as we learned the game along the way.
We would deflated fans be were it not for granddaughter Lori coming on;
Though a sophomore, she is a highly visible player and already well known.
Our Macy we will sorely miss, but we wish her well in her premed college run
And thank her again for teaching us that volleyball games can be such great fun.
Happily, we look forward to three more years of Lori's volleyball play.
That we can continue to make all the games, near and far, we pray.
More and more we sit on the lowest bleacher row;
Up and down steep steps, we are reluctant to go.
Diminished equilibrium and mobility, the dreaded symptoms of old age—
But thank the Lord for grandkids and sports, these symptoms to assuage.

Motherhood, a Universal Phenomenon

A tribute to all mothers

Motherhood is truly a universal phenomenon,
For everyone who is anyone has had one.
And she is praised by both daughter and son,
Even though she may not have been a perfect one.
After all, we don't expect her to act like a nun.
Yes, motherhood is a universal phenomenon.
Motherhood is the ultimate test of womanhood.
A man could not compete even if he would.
Those guys who try must ultimately admit
That only the woman is biologically fit.
For giving birth, she is the only one.
Remember, motherhood is truly a female phenomenon.
Let each of us remember our mother dear
And tell her the things she deserves to hear.
No matter if she be in heaven or in house,
She will savor every kind word from each child's mouth,
Whether they number a dozen or only one.
Yes, motherhood is truly a universal phenomenon.
What are the kind words we need to say?
Why, everything that brushes tears away:
Things that honor her every sacrifice,
That made life for us so very nice,
That made life for us easier and more fun.
Remember, motherhood is truly a universal phenomenon.
Never, ever forget this very special day;
It is your major opportunity to say

Complimentary things that need tongue.
So take care to embellish every single one.
Never allow your mother's heroic deeds to go unsung.
Remember, motherhood is truly a universal phenomenon.
Remember those delicious meals prepared by Mother dear,
Prepared 365 days a year.
Keep in mind that when this special day rolls round,
And she's still here, we take her out on the town,
Take her out to dine, to celebrate, to have fun.
Remember, motherhood is truly a universal phenomenon.
Of course, we could sing praises to our mothers all day long.
But let us not belabor even so fine a song.
Say what sounds best, but say it concisely well,
For everything, time will not allow us to tell.
Anyway, we need a few things to savor all our own.
Remember, motherhood is truly a universal phenomenon.

I Can't Believe Hailey Is Sixteen!

Grandfather (Papa) responds to his granddaughter's sixteenth birthday

Hailey

Seems as if it were only yesterday
When sweet Hailey was in pre-K
But beyond her years academically,
Reading and writing surprisingly,
Making her professor papa swell with pride,
Having an "exceptional" little grand by his side!
Little Hailey and Papa shared a special time;
On designated days they would read and dine.
After her morning at pre-K, Papa would be waiting in line
To accommodate little Hailey's foremost obsession:
Visiting Barnes & Noble for a book-reading session,
Then stopping by Cici's Pizza to complete the mission.
Papa's favorite Hailey story takes place at the Barnes & Noble store,

Where from the beginning he presumed to read to Hailey galore,
Thinking this was the thing to do since little Hailey was only four.
Was he ever surprised, though elated, to hear little Hailey say,
"Papa, let me read to you." Indeed, that was a memorable day!
Papa knew for sure Hailey was an exceptional little pre-K.
Now my little pre-K is sixteen and on the high school and college road.
Somehow this trip down memory lane puts me in a philosophical mode,
So please allow me to pass on a thought to you, Hailey, and to everyone:
At my back, says the poet, I always hear time's winged chariot hurrying near,
And then hastens to add, though we cannot stop the sun, we can make him run.
Meaning utilize time to the fullest—that is to say, make hay while shines the sun.
With that said, Hailey, your Papa wishes you a most happy birthday
And commends you on making that old sun run even while in pre-K.

A Look at Islam

These verses were composed after reading Karen Armstrong's "Islam" and Bernard Lewis's "What Went Wrong."

It all began way back in the year 610;
That's when Muhammad's mysterious revelations began.
He was much disturbed about his Mecca community,
Where he saw wholesale exploitation practiced with immunity.
The rich and strong preyed on the poor and weak;
The tribal code was being ignored by both merchant and sheik.
Spirituality suffered not only in Mecca but in the whole Arab land.
What could save these people of the desert sand?
Why had the high God, Allah, of their pantheon
Not sent the Arabs a prophet or son?
The high God had talked to the Jews and the Christians too;
He had revealed through Scripture what they should do.
Were the Arabs a hopeless and lost people
Without a civilizing synagogue or church steeple?
More than a few people, Arab and non-Arab, harbored such a thought.
For all this skeptical doubt, Muhammad a solution sought
By annually retiring in the month of Ramadan to a cave on a mountain peak,
Where he fasted and prayed for his community to be compassionate and meek.
Then one Ramadan an overwhelming spiritual presence descended upon him,
Pouring torrents of words into his head, filling it to the brim,
Forcing his lips to speak numerous scriptures for Arab ears.
Revelation was at hand for the Arabs who had waited so many years.
And after two years of agonizing secret meditation,

Muhammad went forth proclaiming revelation.
For twenty-two years, the revelations came,
Making Muhammad a prophet of great fame
And spreading Islam throughout the Arabian strand,
Setting the stage for its explosion to the near and the distant land.
Muhammad did not believe he was founding a new religion,
For most of his tribe, Quraysh, who lived in the Mecca region—
And like Jews and Christians—already believed in Creation and judgment,
Even though Allah had not yet a personal prophet to them sent.
But then in 610, their pious Arab brother Muhammad was called,
They believed, to update not only them but Jews, Christians, and all.
The revelations came, chapter by chapter, and filled a book called the Koran,
A book Islam believes to be God's latest and best instruction to man.
The revelations came often in response to a crisis or a question
That provided Muhammad's faithful little community an essential lesson.
These numerous revelations caused the Prophet considerable agony.
"Never," said he, "did I receive a revelation without feeling my soul torn from me."
Yet the confessed agony was only one part of this miraculous mystery
Of how an illiterate prophet could deliver a masterpiece of Arab prose and poetry,
So sublime and powerful to persuade the most sophisticated nonbeliever.
Somehow it softened the hearer's heart, making it a submissive receiver.
That's why it's called Islam, meaning surrender,
And the one who surrenders a Muslim, meaning defender.
Islam began in Mecca but in its infancy could not there survive.
The little community of defenders had to flee in order to stay alive.
The flight, the hegira, relocated them in what became known as Medina, the city—
The city because it was soon transformed into the perfect Islamic society.

Upon arrival, Muhammad celebrated the relocation flight
By building, for Allah, a most holy site.
He constructed the very first mosque, literally a place of prostration,
And provided the model for every future Muslim nation.
Inside, there was a special place for prayer and a special place for preaching;
Outside, there was a courtyard for discourse and beseeching.
In effect, the mosque provided a forum for airing any community concern;
It was a place to worship, to speak, to listen, to learn.
The issue could be religious, political, military issue, or social concern.
The goal of the mosque was unity: to integrate all facets of community life;
To promote brotherhood through shared ideology rather than blood line;
To integrate all of life under the auspices of Allah;
To love all of life by the scripture given Muhammad to follow.
The hegira, the flight to Medina, marks the beginning of the Muslim era;
Here Muhammad implemented a scriptural society, the Koran in mirror,
A mirror that reflected a coveted community across the Arabian strand,
Attracting the support of most tribes throughout the land.
Now triumphant, Muhammad returned to Mecca, the holy city,
To destroy the idols around the Kaaba and dedicate it to Allah.
Henceforth, when pilgrims came to Mecca the Black Stone in the Kaaba to kiss,
It would be to confirm their Muslim faith and to bask for a moment in Allah's bliss.
Muhammad made the Black Stone Allah's very own, whatever its pre-Islamic appeal.
It was the stone that now served as the Islamic holy of holies, and under Allah's seal.
It was the stone that now Muslims must visit once to assure their heavenly reward.

It was the stone that anchored a vibrant force about to become the world's vanguard.
Pouring out of Mecca, the force spread north and east and west;
From its various neighbors, land and power Islam began to wrest:
To the east Iraq submits; to the north and west, Syria and Egypt fall.
And what but to appall both Christian and Jew when Palestine and Jerusalem fall?
The year is now 641, and Muslim armies continue to roll conquering ancient Iran,
Then Cyprus, parts of Pakistan and India, and all of Afghanistan.
In time, much of North Africa and Spain fall under Muslim rule,
As well as much of Eastern Europe, Russia, Southeast Asia, and Istanbul.
From midseventh century through mideighteenth and then some,
The Muslim empire strutted on the stage of world power as number one.
When Islam's original energy from the Arabian peninsula begins to wan,
It is infused with that of vibrant Turkish tribes, the Seljuk and the Ottoman.
From the seventh to the eighteenth century was Islam's great expand,
An expansion that continues, second only to that of the Christian.
Muslims saw their culture high but that of the Christians low.
For instance, they viewed ungodly the Christian crusades to free medieval Palestine
And attributed the Crusaders' eviction to the superior virtues of their heroic Saladin.
They viewed Christian Europe as little more than a barbarian outpost,
While the Islamic empire to learning and culture played sophisticated host.
It had inherited the knowledge and skills of the ancient Middle East;
To that it added more from India and China, from ancient Persia and Greece.
Fusing the cultural richness of the past with its own innovation,
Islam went beyond the high-water mark of any previous civilization.
But viewing Islam clothed in its twenty-first-century raiment,

It's difficult to believe its once envious attainment
When we see backwardness and poverty and radicalism in almost all its lands unfurl,
When we hear radical leaders proclaiming the great Satan to be the Western world,
When we see radicals striking at Israel, America, and the West en masse and alone;
Yet we pray that Christians, Jews, and Islam, Abraham's children, one day get along!

The Coronavirus Pandemic of 2020 and More

These lines were penned in May of 2020.

Who will ever forget that coronavirus pandemic 2020 sent?
From country to country and continent to continent, it went!
Such a devastating plague, a total blank in the memory of all—
Doubtful anyone living could such a ravaging pandemic recall,
Though many might compare it to the bubonic plague of history,
When, mysteriously, rats and fleas became harbingers of misery.
Despite the time and talent in science and technology invested,
Still, several centuries later, a world plague ravages *unarrested*!
Cable television pundits about the virus endlessly speculate;
Scientists and physicians, virus experts, designate, pontificate.
Partisan politicians exploit the crisis for personal and party gain.
John and Jane Doe, desperate and confused, quarantined remain.
Masking and social distancing for now the new social norm:
No handshakes or hugs; keep your distance or cause alarm.
Viral germs, experts declare, permeate the air, we suspect!
Don't breathe them in or out; both yourself and others protect.
Wear your mask ear to ear attached; let it be the dual screen.
Keep your distance; wash your hands; spray and swipe clean.
Many businesses mandated to close; all commerce restricted
By order either of president, governor, or mayor, interdicted.
Workers by the millions on furlough, small businesses sinking!
Government supplements in the trillions; what are leaders thinking?
Which is worse, risking the virus or risking economic disaster?
Both lethal, the question to answer: How both to rationally master?
The answer will require an abundance of prayer and much goodwill.
The crises will not be resolved by crafting some sleazy political deal.

Now is the time to rescue our republic from those who would it eliminate!
John and Jane Doe be not confused, support the commonsense candidate!
Identify all politicos who side step and dissemble before marking your ballot
Now is the time to know whether a candidate has common sense or has not.
The future of our nation relies on common sense prevailing in November;
The second Tuesday of November 2020 will be an election to remember.
Two roads meet on that day at the ballot box: Which will most voters take?
Let us pray that common sense prevails so that the road taken is not a mistake,
That newly elected leaders imbued with common sense set things straight,
That the exemplary permeates their leadership and the coronavirus dissipates.
Conjecture:
Killer viruses, both the physical and the political, are of demonic design
And only controlled by common sense faithfully anchored in the divine.
That is not to say, ignore science and technology—of course not!
It is to say, prayerfully utilize common sense, no matter what!

Things That Matter Most

If you were asked the question, "What things matter most?"
What would be your answer? What would be your post?
Perhaps it is a question on which you have never dwelled,
Thereby being a question that for you does not ring a bell.
Had I not recently rearranged my cluttered attic,
The question may have been for me only static.
But having scanned a stack of rhymed verse neatly stored
Put me in mode inquisitive: "Why did I these things hoard?"
Ironically, I, the author, could not readily say why so—
Surprisingly though, I was engrossed. I wanted to know!
"What is this mysterious, psychological thing I'm feeling now?"
Scanning poems, some decades old, yet so pleasing somehow.
Why were they written at all, and why for so very long?
Why do they linger in my mind like a memorable song?
The motivation was never economic gain; that was plain to see.
Something other it had to be, and that is what truly intrigued me.
After considerable analytical probing and internal chatter, myself the host,
I concluded: "The poems my attempt to freeze in time things that matter most."

Cale, Remembering You on Your Thirtieth Birthday

Celebrating precious memories

A coming event reminds me that time's winged chariot hurries near;
Our second grandson, Caleb, known as Cale, turns thirty this year.
Such a short time ago, I was bouncing the lovable little guy on my knee,
Or so it seems: now Cale, wife Lynne, and baby Sawyer Grace, I see,
Reminding me that time allows pause button none;
It is only through memory that time pause can be done.
And that is what I wish to do:
Relate a few fond memories of you.
Mom Sally was always hovering near first baby Will,
But the two of you, Cale and Will, somehow lowered her zeal,
Allowing grandparents to seize little Cale for a moment or two.
To cuddle and rock, dotingly doing what grands love to do,
And your sweet disposition buoyed your grands immensely;
Your coo and a smile and extended arms thrilled them intensely.
Later on we were taking you to the farm to visit your great grands Dowell,
Truly hoping a short separation from Mom and Dad would not incite a howl.
Happily, you were in big boy mode, no homesick tears as we left Houston behind,
Just a little heartstring tug detected in your response to an observation of mine:
"Cale, look out the window at the pretty moon, big and bright, lighting up the sky."
"Yeah, it's pretty here, but I bet it's bigger and prettier in Houston" was your reply.

And there was the time you visited us in McAllen expecting to choose your fun,
Not knowing your Mom's specific request: "I prefer he not play with any toy gun."
When Nanny took you to the toy store to shop for toys, you spot the desired one.
"The one I've always wanted," you say, "that one too high to reach, the popgun."
When Nanny hesitates, you hastily proclaim, "Mom would sure want me to have it."
Stifling a knowing smile, Nanny replies, "Cale, on the gun we have to wait a bit."
And wait you did, waited for the years ahead and a nonurbanization location,
Where you heard Papa declare, "My grandsons need a little agrarian orientation."
So every time opportune, we stole you away to the farm for a little rural fun,
Feeding cattle, fixing fences, fishing the ponds, hunting and shooting a gun.
Enough of our childhood memories now that you are thirty, and three in one
Processing memories of your own little one, so when grown up will still be young.
Precious memories, how they linger, celebrate the refrain of an old song;
Without memory, the past is gone, and familiarity in the present unknown.
Devouring time erases the past and tells us nothing about the future to come;
Without precious memory, how empty life would most surely be for everyone.
Though we know not what lies ahead, we have blessed memories that serve us well,

Foremost being memories of our family—and today foremost being our grandson Cale.

Remembering When...

One of the joys of being a parent is remembering when.
Most parents love recalling certain events again and again,
More often than not an event with a humorous bent
Something out of the ordinary, something incongruent.
Something when recounted always elicits a little levity,
Be it a long-winded recitation or be it one of brevity.
One of my favorites involves a Christmas tree incident;
Being recently cut, our tree gave off a distinct cedar scent,
Which we assuaged by circling it with a popcorn chain
Before bringing out the icicles and lights and everything.
Beginning with the angel at the top, we decorated the tree all
Except its bottom limbs; each reserved for a little red crystal ball
Our two young sons, Stan and Dwight, were beyond excited,
Especially Dwight, who from a recent birthday still delighted,
Wearing his birthday cowboy boots, his present proud,
Kicking often and high so the bootheels came down loud.
Then suddenly he stood still, gazing at the tree's bottom trim,
Fixated on the little red crystal balls as if mesmerized by them.
Only reluctantly did he leave the tree for the dinner call,
For reason strange he was by the little red balls enthralled.
Soon after the family dined, Dwight was nowhere in sight;
Then I heard coming from the tree room cackles of delight.
I knew that it had to be Dwight and that something wasn't right.
With each cackle came another sound that wasn't from Dwight.
Rushing to the scene, I caught Dwight kicking a shiny red ball,
But he turned around and smiled as if it were nothing at all.
I know you're angry, Dad, about my kicking the Christmas tree.
I don't know what makes me do it, so please don't punish me.
Wait! Wait! I think I do know what makes me kick this tree:

It's these kicker boots, these birthday boots you gave me.
It was all I could do to suppress a knowing smile, for
I heard Adam saying, "It was this woman you made for me."
I heard Eve saying, "It was the serpent who deceived me."
I heard Paul saying, "The good I would do, I do not . .
I heard Flip Wilson saying, "The devil made me do it."
Then I said, "Dwight, let's take off these boots; it's bedtime."

OUR GREAT-GRANDS VISIT THE FARM

Our great-grands having fun at the farm: feeding the cows cubes and fishing at the pond.

"Hey, Papa, may we feed the cows some cubes?" shout my grands great
As they turn around standing on the bottom strand of the pasture gate.
They knew the cows came running when offered something to eat;
Three or four cows had arrived already, anticipating a tasty treat.
It only took one meeting for kids and cows to become friends sweet.
The cows were lured to the gate by four little hands, each holding a cube;

When a cow came close with open mouth, a cube was poked in like in a tube.
The constant laughter and shrills of joy left no doubt feeding cows was great fun,
But as soon as the cubes were gone, Papa heard, "May we go fishing in the pond?"
"Of course you may," came the answer from their doting great-grand,
Though he knew that required preparing fishing tackle and a caravan,
Rods and reels, and lures galore, and vehicles for transporting the crew,
For the crew would be not only the great-grandkids but their parents too:
Parents to serve as driver, gate opener, backlash fixer, cheerleader, and fish netter.
A well-trained parent fish caddy; a well-stocked pond: fishing doesn't get any better.
The fish wagon visits twice a year to assure the fish stay healthy and the water clear.
Papa, thinking ahead, had turned a pasture into a hay meadow and enlarged the pond.
"I want my grandkids and great-grandkids to have a place to fish free of cattle dung,"
He said, "but there's one thing unchanged: we shall catch and release as always done."
And release they did, but not before each catch was videoed thoroughly,
Bass striking frequently, kids reeling excitedly, parents assisting proudly
Cell phones videoing constantly, great-grandkids excited ecstatically.
A backlash now and then diminished euphoria but only temporarily,
Papa pacing to and fro, thanking heaven above for his precious family to host
And for the God-given longevity to enjoy these blessed things that matter most.

Author Biography

Dr. Bob (PhD) brings an engaging freshness to traditional biblical thought through creative utilization of genre: poetry in *Understanding the Bible: Head and Heart*; drama in *Papa, Tell Us about the Bible*; dialogue in *Satan and Me and OBE*. And in *What Makes America Great*, he presents a narrative laced with evidence from representative literary and historical documents confirming the country's exemplary founding and its continued pursuit of the exemplary—life, liberty, and pursuit of happiness—for all its people.

Made in the USA
Monee, IL
14 February 2021